# THE
# NAZI
# War Machine

*'There can only be one victor, and that is us . . .'*

# THE
# NAZI
# War Machine

ES KANN NUR EINER
SIEGEN UND DAS
SIND WIR

GOTTFRIED KLEIN    ADOLF HITLER AM 8. NOVEMBER 1939

TIGER BOOKS INTERNATIONAL
LONDON

This edition published in 1996 by
Tiger Books International PLC, Twickenham

© Graham Beehag Books, Christchurch, Dorset

Printed in Singapore by Star Standard Industries Pte. Ltd.

ISBN 1-85501-830-6

# CONTENTS

# INTRODUCTION

It is now more than 50 years since the death of Adolf Hitler and the destruction of the Third Reich he tried to establish as a thousand-year empire, but the subject of Hitler and the Nazi party, together with the military machine they created for the pursuance of their imperial ambitions, is still one of enduring fascination. This fascination results in part from an attempt to understand the political, economic, social and psychological factors that created this aberrant force in modern European history, and in part from the continuing horror still felt about the vast evils perpetrated by the Nazi regime in its attempts to secure Lebensraum (living space) in eastern Europe by the conquest and wholesale subjugation of countries such as Poland and the western part of the USSR, and to 'cleanse' its empire of the political, intellectual, social and, most devastatingly of all, racial groups that would otherwise taint the 'Aryan' future of Germany.

Thus it is the total destructiveness of Hitler's regime, which lasted only 12 years between 1933 and 1945, that fascinates. In this time the Nazis and their allies managed to unleash largest war of all history, and in the process firstly shattered for a time at least the unity of Germany, which had been one of the great political achievements of the 19th century; secondly upset the balance of power in Europe and thereby facilitated the emergence of the USA and USSR as the two great superpowers; and thirdly destroyed the concept of European superiority in Africa and Asia, thereby opening the way for the dissolution of the European empires (especially those of France and the UK, with those of Belgium, Spain and Portugal following).

There are thus two major aspects to the history of Hitler and his Third Reich in the form of the plans for and implementation of the Nazis' political and racial policies, with particularly emphasis on 'ethnic cleansing' by euthanasia or genocide, and of the huge development and deployment of German military strength. These two factors were inextricably intertwined at the highest levels of the German politico-military machine's chaotic grand strategic thinking, but this book is concerned with the nature of the military machine as such.

This military machine had survived in truncated form from the end of World War I (1914-18), the sensible plans of its general staffs being the preservation of current military skills in combination with a pioneering operational analysis of Germany's failings in World War I and the inculcation of high levels of personal skills so that the men of these currently small armed forces could become that cadre on which substantially larger forces could be developed quickly and efficiently as soon as the relevant political, economical and industrial factors were present. Throughout the 1920s, clandestine weapons development and training had been undertaken, the former with the aid of subsidiaries of German companies in Italy, Spain, Sweden, Switzerland and the USSR, and the latter at the training establishments which Germany had secured in the USSR in exchange for German technical assistance in the

*Adolf Hitler was generally able to secure a moral and psychological superiority over the staffs of the German armed forces, which were selected for pliability and administrative capability rather than outright strength of character and proven military skills.*

development of Soviet military capabilities. Limited expansion of the German armed forces was already under way in clandestine fashion even before the rise of the Nazi party to power in 1933, but from this time expansion and re-equipment proceeded more rapidly and less covertly than before until the time in 1935 when the Nazi party signalled Germany abrogation of the restrictions imposed on it by the Treaty of Versailles that had in 1919 ended Germany's part in World War I.

Through the 1930s, the planning of Germany's military leaders had coincided with the timetable of the German political leadership in postulating no outbreak of hostilities before 1942, and this was particularly important to the navy, which had been harder hit by the Treaty of Versailles than the army, and required proportionally longer time to prepare the designs for new warships, built them and finally bring them into effective service with properly trained crews. The same should have applied on a slightly smaller scale to the air force as Germany's possession for such a service had been specifically banned by the Treaty of Versailles, but the clandestine formulation of the air force had been a simpler matter than the establishment of a larger and more capable navy, and the provision of the right types of warplanes had been a quicker matter once the Nazi leadership had decided that air power was a simple way for the German forces to achieve parity with and then superiority over its European military rivals.

Despite the intention of the military and political leadership not to essay any major military undertaking before 1942, Hitler committed Germany to World War II (1939-35) three years early for a number of psychological as well as politico-military reasons. The German leader's primary military consideration was the desire to exploit the capabilities of the newly created German war machine at a time it still enjoyed a manifest superiority, in technology and trained numbers, over the forces of France and the UK. These two countries, which had been primarily responsible for the defeat of Germany in World War I, were expanding and re-equipping their armed forces at an accelerating rate, and Hitler decided that Germany should secure its primary objectives before France and the UK could intervene effectively, in which case they might be persuaded to accept the new order in Europe without entering a large-scale conflict with Germany.

Hitler was also persuaded that an early start to hostilities was dictated by his desire to settle matters with France and the UK before turning his attention to the east, where the destruction of the USSR was his main politico-military objective. All too aware of the problems that the fighting of a two-front war had caused Germany in World War I, Hitler sensibly decided that France and the UK would therefore have to be neutralised before he unleashed his forces on the USSR, and that this latter event should take place no later than the spring or summer of 1941, when the Soviet forces might reasonably be expected to start regaining a measure of real strength after a major re-equipment programme and after the effects of the purging of its officer corps in the late 1930s had been overcome.

These and other factors persuaded Hitler to go to war in 1939 when he had a major superiority of tactical power for *Blitzkrieg* (lightning war) in the cohesive strength of his new and unrivalled Panzer divisions under the air umbrella that could be provided by the Luftwaffe's tactical air power, which had been tested and perfected by support for the Nationalist forces in the Spanish Civil War (1936-39). In the short term, Hitler's reasoning was correct: Poland fell after a short but sharp fight in September 1939, Denmark and Norway were invaded in April 1940, and in May the German forces poured into the Netherlands, Belgium and France. By the end of June 1940s all these countries were under German control, the British had pulled back to their own country as the sole opponent left in the war, and Italy had entered the arena on Germany's side.

Then it all started to go wrong for Germany. Designed for tactical support of the ground forces, the Luftwaffe failed to beat the Royal Air Force in the Battle of Britain and thereby pave the way for a German invasion of the UK, the *Blitz* bombing campaign against British cities failed to bring the UK to its knees, Italy's ill-starred campaign against the British in North Africa was running into difficulties from which the Germans were forced to rescue them, and the Balkan states of Yugoslavia and Greece were seen as threat that had to be neutralised before the German forces invaded the USSR. The were a number of successes, such as the U-boat and surface raider campa against British merchant shipping, that provided encouragement for Ger military planners, but the fact remained that the UK was still in the war, was providing a liability rather than an asset, and the diversion to Yugos

*The Focke-Wulf Fw 190 was one of the finest warplanes built in Germany during World War II, and although designed as a general-purpose fighter with a radial-engined powerplant as seen here, it was soon developed into a multi-faceted fighter-bomber, attack fighter, reconnaissance platform and torpedo strike fighter with either a radial- or Vee-engined powerplant.*

and Greece had delayed the start of the campaign against the USSR from spring to the summer of 1941.

The initial success of the Soviet campaign was enormous, and as a result it seemed that Germany was at the height of its power. With hindsight, however, it is possible to see that Germany was already past the peak of its military capabilities at all but the tactical level, for what Hitler and his increasingly cowed military advisers refused to consider were two seminal facts. The first of these was the fact that Germany was not prepared for a long war, and that despite the current growth on Soviet military capabilities, it would have been desirable to postpone the invasion of the USSR to the spring of 1942 so that Germany would have had an additional nine months or more to put its war industries and recruitment/training efforts onto a total war basis, which was as yet not even considered, while the second was the fact that Germany was now embarking on a two-front war with a hard-hit but certainly not defeated UK is its rear and actively pursuing a policy not only of building up its own strength and capabilities, but also of seeking to establish a coalition of anti-German nations including, most importantly of all, the USA with its huge manpower and industrial resources.

Hitler believed, however, that the USSR would be defeated before the end of 1941, for his concept of war was embodied in the Blitzkrieg, in which a series of sudden campaigns would be fought, each living off the spoils of the previous campaign and achieving overwhelming success with strictly limited matériel resources whose maintenance would present no undue burden to the German people. This concept had worked in the time of Germany's great initial successes, but wholly ignored the fact that the USSR was an altogether more formidable opponent that was quite willing to lose vast numbers of men and machines as it retreated back into its hinterland to recoup its strength from virtually limitless manpower resources and a rebuilt industrial capability.

The fallacy of Hitler's concept became apparent with the German armies' failure to defeat the USSR by the end of 1943 and their continued failure to achieve this same objective during 1942, when more territorial gains were made but without inflicting decisive damage on Soviet forces that were, in the last stages of the year, to trap the German 6th Army in Stalingrad. In combination with the almost simultaneous British victory over the Germans and Italians at El Alamein in North Africa, this marked the beginning of the end for Germany_s military plans. In the summer of 1943 the British and Americans landed in Sicily as a precursor to an invasion of Italy, Allied forces were massing in the UK for a descent on northern France, and Germany irretrievably lost the strategic initiative on the Eastern Front.

It was only after these events that Hitler, who was still refusing to believe the real nature of the situation and perhaps even believing his own propaganda machine's assertion that Germany had long been waging total war, was finally persuaded to permit a shift of Germany's stance to that required for total war. Thus is was only in the middle of 1944, when World War II was already lost, that Germany finally developed total mobilisation of its human and industrial resources for a war that had now become one of attrition. Faced with the USSR on one side and the combination of Britain and the USA on the other, Germany could not hope to win this type of war in either manpower or matériel terms.

Despite the inevitability of a German defeat from this time onwards, it was to be May 1945 before the end finally came. Even though this Nazi refusal to bow to the inevitable led to the extensive casualties and destruction that took place in the last nine months of the war, it is nonetheless a telling indication of the capabilities of the German fighting man. It is arguable that no one excelled the average German infantryman, airman or submariner in basic fighting determination and skill on one-to-one terms, and the German fighting machine was therefore a superb one at the tactical level. It was also excellent at the operational level. Above this level, however, the quality of the German war machine declined rapidly. Many strategic masterpieces were conceived and executed by senior German commanders during World War II, but there were also a number of very poorly planned strategic efforts, especially when Hitler and his immediate military subordinates intervened.

Until 1938, the German military machine had been a wholly professional organisation with each of the armed forces headed by a senior officer receiving political direction from the Nazi government. In the spring of 1938, however, Hitler dismissed General Werner von Blomberg as his

*The 'pocket battleship' Graf Spee was a dedicated commerce raider designed specifically to roam for long periods, extended by resupply from supporting ships at prearranged rendezvous points, on the maritime lines of communications required by the UK and, to a lesser extent, by France. To this end the ship was spaciously laid out for maximum habitability, the propulsion arrangement was based on diesel engines for moderately high speed but very long range, and the gun primary gun armament was six 11in (280mm) guns in two triple turrets.*

minister of war and assumed his responsibilities with the aid of Generaloberst Wilhelm Keitel, the chief of the Oberkommando der Wehrmacht (Armed Forces High Command) or OKW which, despite its title, was merely an advisory body with no authority over the Oberkommando des Heeres (OKH), Oberkommando der Kriegsmarine (OKK) and Oberkommando der Luftwaffe (OKL), which were the three separate high command organisations whose commanders-in-chief and chiefs-of-staff were not organised in any overall grand strategic team but met merely at Hitler's orders to receive his direct instructions.

In the late summer of 1940, for example, Hitler and Keitel were in Berchtesgaden in southern Germany, the rest of the OKW staff was at Potsdam near Berlin, which was also the location of the bulk of the OKL, the OKM was in Berlin, and the OKH was at Zossen south of Berlin. This lack of physical and operational co-ordination reflected Hitler's belief in his own genius as a strategic planner, and his distrust of professional military men.

The lack of co-ordination and collaboration at the highest military levels was also typical of the politico-military level, where the Germans lacked anything resembling the American or British 'war cabinets'. Hitler's cabinet had its last meeting in 1938, and although a Reichsverteidigungsrat (Reich Defence Council) was established with Hitler as chairman and Hermann Goering as his deputy, this soon fell into abeyance even though political figures as senior as Joseph Goebbels and Albert Speer, respectively the propaganda and armament ministers, asked Goering to revive it in the period after the loss of the 6th Army at Stalingrad in February 1943.

This direct control of the German military machine was exercised from the *Wolfsschanze* (wolf's lair) in East Prussia by Hitler assisted by Keitel, Martin Bormann and Hans Lammers, the last two being Hitler's Nazi party deputy and state secretary respectively.

# DAS HEER

In 1919 Germany was forced to sign the Treaty of Versailles to conclude its losing part in World War I, and in this the victorious Allies sought to ensure that Germany would never again be capable of fighting an aggressive war. One of the main limitations imposed on Germany by the treaty, therefore, was an army numbering no more than 100,000 men (three cavalry and seven infantry divisions) with no water-cooled machine guns, heavy artillery or armoured vehicles. All 100,000 of this new Reichsheer were to be volunteers rather than conscripts, moreover, and Germany was also prohibited from the import of any weapons.

What the treaty could not prevent was the carefully fostered belief that the defeat of Germany in World War I was in no way attributable to the German army as such but rather to failures elsewhere in Germany. Small and increasingly efficient as a result of its leanness, the German army therefore had great pride in itself and trained hard under the leadership of Generaloberst Hans von Seeckt's general staff which, unaccountably, the Allies had not sought to eliminate despite its manifest skills in running the German land war in World War I.

The officers and men of the Reichsheer were taught to believe in themselves as true professionals who were maintaining the ethos and skills of the German army pending the time that they could inculcate these into the new and larger army that would emerge once Germany had been freed from the shackles of Versailles. Thus the Reichsheer was seen from its beginning as the nucleus from which a greater army would evolve, and in parallel with this legal force there were several organisations that broke the spirit if not the law of Versailles: shooting clubs helped to train young men in the skills of marksmanship and the comradely nature of the soldier, for example, while demobilisation and welfare organisations provided a network through which mobilisation could be effected and trained men recalled to the colours. Officers were sent on fact-finding trips to other countries for the purposes of keeping themselves and their brother officers as up to date as possible with the latest military thinking and hardware, and amongst the most important of these foreign visits were those made by young officers such as Heinz Guderian and other 'tank enthusiasts' to the Soviet tank training centre at Kazan.

*Profiting from operational lessons learned the hard way from Soviet tanks such as the T-34, the PzKpfw V Panther was Germany's finest tank of World War II for its excellent blend of firepower, protection and mobility. It was fortunate for the Allies and the Soviets that German industry did not produce this type sooner and in larger quantities, for it was a truly excellent fighting machine.*

Another aspect of Germany's endeavours to keep up with the latest thinking in weapons technology was the use of foreign subsidiaries or allies to produce and test prototype weapons. In the 1920s, for instance, Krupp detached to Bofors, a Swedish company, a team of artillery designers who returned to Germany in 1931 with the plans for a highly capable 88mm (3.465in) anti-aircraft gun that became a classic dual-role anti-aircraft and anti-tank weapon in World War II.

Perhaps the most important contribution made by the Reichsheer to the army of the Third Reich was the creation of leaders at every level, with leadership seen as a result of individual skill and personality rather than a by-product of breeding from the German aristocracy. In the 1920s the Reichsheer established an army psychology research institute, and this played an important part in developing within the army the notion that every man, from the highest-ranking officer to the private soldier, must be capable of thinking for himself so that he could use his initiative rather than blindly adhere to orders that had reached him along the chain of command. A more egalitarian influence became evident in the army, which thus began to pay more attention to officers who had displayed leadership and initiative qualities than to those who had merely been 'bred' to the role.

It is therefore arguable that the Reichsheer, instead of becoming the small defence-oriented service intended by the Treaty of Versailles, became the extremely highly trained and very capable cadre of a new army or, as opined by one British officer, 'the reinforcement, the steel frame, onto which the concrete of conscripts could quickly be poured, if and when it became possible to reintroduce conscription'.

By the early 1930s, the Reichsheer was ready and waiting for expansion and, despite its traditional opposition to any interference in national politics, now began to play an active part in the Nazi party's rise to power, probably for lack of any realistic alternative to Adolf Hitler. The president of Germany was already an army officer, the legendary Generalfeldmarschall Paul von Hindenburg, and the chancellor and war minister were also army officers,

*Although it aroused a measure of indulgent ridicule as well as anxiety in the countries bordering on Germany, the pageantry of the Nazi party was a decisive element in pulling Germany together behind Hitler and his regime in the early and mid-1930s.*

namely General Kurt von Schleicher and General Werner von Blomberg, the latter being appointed to his position with a secret mandate to ensure that there was no army opposition to the appointment of Hitler as chancellor in succession to von Schleicher. Hitler was able to secure the approval of the army, most of whose officers despised this 'jumped-up corporal' of Austrian origins, by playing on its need for approval and constantly averring that the army was the true 'sword bearer' of the nation.

In January 1933 Hitler became chancellor; in the following month the German constitution's seven guarantees of individual and civil liberties were suspended; in July the Nazi party became the only legal

*Watched by Hermann Goering (front left), Adolf Hitler greets the aged German chancellor, Generalfeldmarschall Paul von Hindenburg, at the time of the Nazis' accession to power. Hindenburg, who was soon to die, had a very low opinion of Hitler and his subordinates.*

political party in Germany; in June 1934 the army "looked the other way" when the Nazis purged their own stable by crushing the power of its *Sturmabteilungen* (the SA 'brown-shirts' who were its political street-fighting 'army' in the so-called 'night of the Long Knives'); upon the death of von Hindenburg in August, Hitler was acclaimed as Führer (leader), combining in his own person the roles of Reich president and chancellor, and the recipient of the oath of allegiance was changed from the state to the Führer.

In March 1935, with his power in Germany fully consolidated with the tacit approval of the army, Hitler announced Germany's renunciation of the terms imposed by the Treaty of Versailles, the creation of a new German air force as the Luftwaffe, and the reintroduction of conscription to allow the creation of a 36-division army. This last fact astonished the army, which had never considered a first-stage expansion to more than 21 divisions. Hitler was determined to waste no time, and in May 1935 army planners were instructed to begin work on the first military move demanded by Hitler,

namely the remilitarisation of the Rhineland, whose demilitarisation had been one of the clauses of the Treaty of Versailles.

By this time, the efforts of the armour enthusiasts within the German army had yielded impressive results with dummy tanks, in theory at least, and Hitler saw the opportunity to combine advanced German tactical thinking (albeit derived ultimately from British ideas) with the developing capability of German industry in the creation of a weapon that would offer the German army a decisive tactical advantage over its potential enemies, which were all concerning themselves with exploiting the lessons of World War I rather than looking into the future.

With the active support of the Nazi party, the German army created its first three Panzer divisions in 1935, and in a successful effort to tack the new type of weapon onto the existing framework, the most experienced cavalry regiments were selected for early conversion to the tank. Initially, the Panzer divisions existed on paper rather than in reality pending the delivery of their first true tanks, but this fact did not prevent Hitler from taking the first of many military gambles when he ordered the reoccupation of the Rhineland in March 1936. At this time the French had a considerably larger and better-equipped army than the Germans despite the latter's rapid

*Left: A key element in moulding support for the Nazi party was the enrolment of many thousands of young persons in the party's Hitler Jugend and allied youth movements. Here, in their impressionable adolescence, these persons could be indoctrinated with a passionate belief in the party as embodied in Hitler.*

*Flanked by party dignitaries also wearing the 'brown-shirt' uniform complete with breeches and knee boots, Hitler rose to power with the aid of the uniformed* Sturmabteilungen, *or SA, which were the Nazis' street-fighting units under the command of Ernst Röhm, who was Hitler's only rival to supreme power until he was 'purged' in 1934.*

rearmament and expansion, and it has often been argued that a major French response to this German move could have prevented Hitler's further consolidation of power. Hitler felt that he knew the mood of France at this time, especially as Italy's far more aggressive war against Abyssinia (1935-36) had elicited from the international community no more than cross words and a limited trade embargo, and Hitler also timed the German move to coincide with a French preoccupation with the decision to sign a mutual aid agreement with the USSR.

At dawn on 7 March 1936, one German division moved into the Rhineland with orders to withdraw at once should the French intervene, but after two days it was clear that the French lacked the nerve for any such riposte and Hitler could claim that his strategic vision, which he later described as *schlaffwandlerisches Sicherheit* (the assurance of a sleepwalker), had pulled off a miraculous 'victory' for Germany over the doubts of the generals. From this point onwards, therefore, Hitler began to gain over the generals a moral ascendancy that he was never to lose.

Further expansion and rearmament of the army continued in 1936 and 1937, and towards the end of 1937 another incident occurred that helped to boost Hitler's strength *vis-à-vis* the army. In November 1937 Hitler informed the army high command that war was inevitable, and that as first steps in the expansion of Germany he proposed the seizure of Austria and Czechoslovakia. The generals were astounded, and Hitler received protests from Blomberg and General Werner Freiherr von Fritsch, the commander-in-chief, that such moves were impossible given the army's current lack of real strength as it sought to consolidate after the inevitable disruptions of its recent growth and re-equipment. Hitler's response to these objections was rapid and forceful: both officers were driven into retirement on trumped-up charges, although Fritsch was later cleared of homosexuality but not reinstated.

Hitler capitalised on the temporary absence of army opposition to establish his own command structure, the Oberkommando der Wehrmacht with himself at the head with Generaloberst Wilhelm Keitel as chief-of-staff and later General Alfred Jodl as chief of operations.

In the early spring of 1938 Hitler saw an opportunity for the swift annexation of Austria, and after an extremely rapid and somewhat chaotic planning and preparation period, marked by difficulties with the fuel supplies for the Panzer units, the Germans moved into Austria on 12 March 1938, fortunately for themselves meeting no opposition. Austria was annexed into the 'Greater German Reich', and Hitler was once again able to claim the credit for a great and bloodless victory.

Hitler's next target was Czechoslovakia, which was now surrounded on three sides by German-held territory but possessed a capable army and powerful fixed defences in the Sudetenland, which were the border areas peopled largely by a population of German ethnic origins. Hitler's first gambit was therefore to demand the 'return' to Germany of the Sudetenland, whose loss would leave Czechoslovakia effectively defenceless. Czechoslovakia refused this request, but the threat of war in central Europe spreading to other areas persuaded the British and French to intervene, resulting in the Munich agreement of September 1938 whereby Germany stated that the Sudetenland marked the end of its territorial ambitions in Europe. France and Britain accepted this German lie and, left without support, Czechoslovakia was compelled to cede the Sudetenland.

The possibility of war over Austria and then Czechoslovakia perturbed the army immensely, and General Ludwig Beck, army chief-of-staff under Generaloberst Fedor von Brauchitsch (successor to Fritsch as army commander-in-chief), tried to foment army resistance to Hitler's ambitious plans. Failing to secure any significant support, Beck was forced into retirement and replaced by General Franz Halder, who reflected the army's general mood not of displeasure with Hitler's aggressions but rather of relief that the army would not have to fight its way through the Sudetenland defences. Halder proved a suitable replacement for Beck in the short term, for while he lacked his predecessor's considerable intellect, he was an altogether more practical officer who possessed the ability to translate new ideas into practical methods of warfare.

In March 1939, the rump of Czechoslovakia disappeared as the Slovaks were persuaded to set up a notionally independent Slovakia as a German

*The PzKpfw IV was built in larger numbers than any other German tank of World War II, and as initially planned was the fire-support tank for the PzKpfw III medium battle tank. As the PzKpfw III became obsolete, however, the PzKpfw IV emerged as the German army's principal battle tank of the mid-war years with steadily thicker armour, a main gun of larger calibre and greater barrel length, and modestly improved power.*

client, and the Germans marched into the last part of the former Czechoslovakia on the pretext that the ethnic Germans of the area needed protection. This move shortened Germany's frontier by some 700 miles (1,125km) and also gave the German forces access to some of the best-equipped and most productive armament and vehicle manufacturers in Europe, as well as enough captured tanks to allow the creation of another three Panzer divisions.

Hitler's attention was now focused on Poland, and here the army was again thrown into near-panic: Poland was allied with France and the UK, any German invasion of Poland would surely trigger the major European war that had hitherto been avoided, and a combined British and French declaration of war would surely result in a two-front war as an Anglo-French

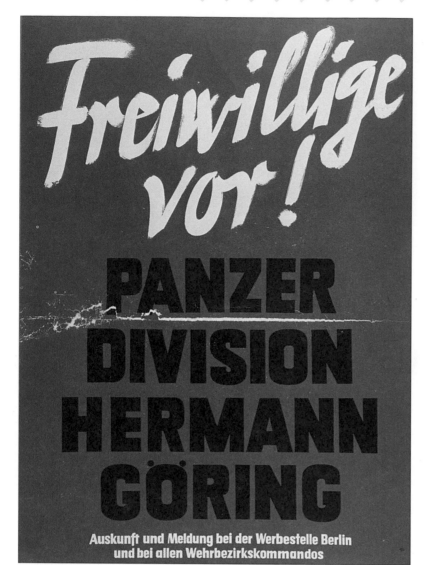

Auskunft und Meldung bei der Werbestelle Berlin
und bei allen Wehrbezirkskommandos

*A German poster calls for volunteers for the Herman nGoering Panzer Division, which was manned entirely by German volunteers, was part of the Luftwaffe, and was an honorary parachute division. The formation saw service in the closing stages of the North African campaign during 1943 and then in Italy up to June 1944, when it was redeployed to the Eastern Front.*

offensive punched through the Westwall or 'Siegfried Line' that had been touted as Germany's main western defence but which was as yet wholly incomplete. Hitler refused even to discuss the non-existence of the Westwall, and then defused the worst fears of the army in August 1939 by signing a non-aggression pact with the USSR, which would now seize the eastern part of Poland after the Germans had invaded from the west, and thereby make it impossible for France or the UK to intervene directly.

On 1 September 1939, therefore, the day on which Germany invaded Poland and started World War II, the German army was relatively content. It knew that it had the strength to complete the rapid conquest of western Poland without depleting the forces holding its western frontiers against the possibility of French and British attack, whereupon there was every likelihood that the British and French would see reason and end hostilities on the basis of the status quo.

In basic military terms, the German army of this period was more capable than most European armies in terms of its offensive power, resulting largely from its possession of six Panzer divisions, four light divisions (soon proved to be largely ineffective and therefore used as the basis for additional Panzer divisions) and four motorised divisions. This force of 14 core divisions gave the army considerable tactical and operational mobility, even though the rest of the army was still largely reliant on horse transport for movement of men, equipment and supplies, and even for the movement of artillery. With the combination of the strategic initiative, the ability to undertake a rapid mobilisation to complete the manning of the army's current strength of 53 divisions, the availability of a first-rate tactical air element, and the *Blitzkrieg* tactics that emphasised deep penetrations by the mobile forces in large-scale pincer movements to disrupt the enemy's defences that would then be dealt with by the slower-moving artillery-supported infantry, the German army possessed every reason to believe that the Polish campaign offered only a very modest threat to German long-term security.

As events in Poland proved during September 1939, the German army was indeed able to achieve stunning victories with great speed and with only modest losses, including many vehicles that could then be recovered, repaired and placed back into service. The same basic tactical and operational method, with the Luftwaffe's tactical air arm serving as 'flying artillery' for the Panzer forces that constituted the deep-plunging spearheads as the infantry followed in their wake with the support of horse-drawn artillery, worked admirably in the period up to December 1941, when the German army was finally halted on the very threshold of Moscow and then, for the first time in World War II, driven back. These 27 months were the

*Hitler receives the accolades of the party faithful in the course of a street parade through a German city. Such events were common during the 1930s, and as such were telling indications of the magnetic effect of Hitler's personality.*

*A German anti-tank team in action with its 37mm PaK 35 towed anti-tank gun. Although obsolescent in its primary role by 1941, this light equipment was kept in service as it was easy to move, and offered considerable secondary capability against targets such as field fortifications.*

period of the German army's greatest offensive triumphs. Part of this success was attributable to the Germans' generally superior equipment, especially in tanks and artillery, whilst the various opposing forces often failed to group their tanks (which were sometimes superior to the opposing German vehicles) into the homogeneous formations whose vigorous counterattacks might have been able to blunt if not halt the progress of the Panzer divisions and thereby check the momentum of the German offensives.

The German successes of the period should not be allowed to disguise the fact that serious problems were already manifesting themselves. The most important of these concerned the slow rate at which damaged or broken-down vehicles were recovered and returned to service, and the increasingly bitter squabbles between the Panzer and infantry generals about the best employment of the tank force. The Panzer generals argued that their tanks could make their greatest contribution by punching through the enemy's defences in operationally large single or double envelopments and then, ignoring the large enemy forces in their rear, by pushing into the enemy's rear areas to disrupt the movement of reinforcements and cut the enemy's lines of communication. This left the following infantry and artillery with the task of grinding down the large enemy pockets left in the Panzers' wake, and in this task they demanded armoured support even if this meant the loss of deep penetration by the Panzer divisions. Hitler sided with the Panzer generals, and the *Blitzkrieg* continued without major operational change.

Yet the German armies did not have things all their own way at the tactical level, and here its generals revealed a steadily growing skill at improvised operations. The most notable of these, in the early stages of World War II, was the excellent way in which Generaloberst Gerd von Rundstedt, commanding Army Group 'South' of the Polish campaign, handled his forces when the Poles made an unexpected and major break-out attempt from the Bzura pocket to the west of Warsaw.

The success of the Polish campaign persuaded Hitler that a rapid switch of the German forces from east to west would allow them to undertake a major offensive in the last part of 1939 against the slowly growing but quiescent British and French strength in eastern France. The army managed to persuade the German leader that redeployment would take too long and that there were inadequate ammunition stocks to support another major offensive, so the offensive was pushed back into the spring of the following year, when the army planned a repeat of the 'Schlieffen Plan' of 1914: a huge offensive into northern France with the German right-wing armies passing to the west of Paris to trap the Allied armies. This was a wholly unimaginative

*The PzKpfw III medium tank was the primary weapon of the Panzer divisions in the early part of World War II. The type was adequately rather than well armoured and had good mobility, but was never more than indifferently armed with a 37mm that was later replaced by a 50mm gun or, in some close support models, a short-barrelled 75mm gun.*

plan, and one which the Allies believed that the Germans would adopt, and a quite brilliant alternative was developed by General Erich von Manstein, von Rundstedt's chief-of-staff, for an armoured punch through the 'impassable' Ardennes in southern Belgium. This major armoured effort would then race to the south coast of the English Channel, cutting off the British and a major part of the French forces from the rest of France and allowing their piecemeal destruction before the Germans turned south and destroyed the rest of the French forces. Halder and von Brauchitsch thoroughly disapproved of this daring plan and managed to suppress it until January 1940, when Hitler learned of it and, immediately appreciating its strategic brilliance, ordered its implementation.

The attack on France, which necessitated the reduction of the Netherlands and Belgium to remove any threat to the Germans' right wing, was delayed by Hitler's last-minute decision to overrun Denmark and Norway in April 1940. Denmark was only a stepping-stone to Norway, which was needed as the route along which vital imports of Swedish iron ore could reach Germany; it offered ports from which German ships could sortie into the North Atlantic to cripple the merchant fleet on which Britain was wholly reliant for the arrival of food, fuel and raw materials; and it would otherwise be occupied by the Allies as a threat to Germany's northern flank. The plan suited the German navy but was little more than an annoying distraction to the army, which currently had some 136 divisions waiting to descend on the Netherlands, Belgium and France. This force included 10 Panzer divisions, of which seven were allocated to the command of General Ewald von Kleist for the main thrust through the Ardennes: the plan was for this force, divided into three Panzer corps, to cross the River Meuse between Sedan in the south and Dinant in the north before striking out to the west in an effort to reach the English Channel coast just to the north of the River Somme's estuary at Abbeville.

The offensive began on 10 May 1940 and achieved overwhelming success. The Netherlands fell without undue difficulty to the two armies of Generaloberst Fedor von Bock's Army Group 'B' supported by pioneering

*Despite the wholly mechanised nature of the Panzer divisions and their support elements, on which the very concept of Blitzkrieg was based, the bulk of the German army was in fact less motorised than the armies of many other European countries. Animal power was therefore very important in the progress of the infantry divisions, artillery units and supply elements following in the wake of the Panzer divisions.*

and well-executed Luftwaffe airborne operations; Belgium fell to one army of Army Group 'B' and two armies of Generaloberst Gerd von Rundstedt's Army Group 'A', again with Luftwaffe airborne support in breaching the Belgians' main defence line; and the 50 divisions along France's fixed defences, namely the Maginot Line, were checked by the 19 infantry divisions of Generaloberst Wilhelm Ritter von Leeb's Army Group 'C'. This left the bulk of Army Group 'B' to drive the 'Panzer corridor' through to the English Channel coast by 20 May, dividing the Allies into two groupings. Virtually every senior commander between von Kleist and Hitler was initially amazed and then concerned by the speed of the unsupported Panzer advance, but General Heinz Guderian saw the Allies' lack of ability to respond and plunged ahead with his XIX Panzer Corps, with XLI and XV Panzer Corps moving slightly more slowly to his north, regardless of orders to mitigate his speed and await support.

The Netherlands and Belgium were driven to capitulation, while most of the British and many of the French in the northern grouping were evacuated to England from Dunkirk by 4 June after Hitler had refused to allow the Panzer forces to reduce this pocket when Hermann Goering claimed that his Luftwaffe could complete the destruction of the area. Spearheaded by the Panzergruppen von Kleist and Guderian, each containing two Panzer corps, the Germans then turned their attention south, advancing over the River Somme to take Paris (declared an open city to avoid destruction), and then driving deep into central and south-western France before France capitulated in an armistice that came into force on 25 June.

The offensive was an enormous success, but also a success that had been bought only at considerable cost including large numbers of tanks, which could not rapidly be replaced if they were incapable of repair, as well as

*A German poster exhorts the German people with impressive illustrations of the sterling qualities of their fighting men.*

25

27,100 men killed, 111,000 wounded and 18,200 initially declared missing but later discovered to be dead.

Hitler now had to decide on his next move: the army needed a time for rest and rehabilitation, the navy was incapable of immediate action as a result of its very high losses in the Norwegian campaign, and the Luftwaffe's airborne arm also needed reconstruction (and also expansion) after its losses in the Dutch and Belgian operations. The army and navy were ordered to co-operate in the preparation of the 'Seelöwe' (sea lion) plan for an amphibious landing on the southern coast of Britain (which steadfastly refused German offers of peace), and in the meantime the Luftwaffe was to undertake the destruction of the Royal Air Force's Fighter Command so that the invasion could proceed under an undisturbed umbrella of German tactical warplanes.

This action started the Battle of Britain, which the vainglorious Goering assured Hitler would result in a rapid and conclusive victory for his Luftwaffe. In fact, the result was Germany's first defeat of World War II, and Hitler turned aside from his plan to invade and conquer the UK in favour of his longer-term objective of crushing the USSR and totally destroying the Soviet political system.

The plan was for the invasion of the USSR to begin in the spring of 1941, but dangerous delay resulted from the need for German forces to move into the Balkans, where Italy's attempt to crush Greece had been disastrous and

*When Germany seized the rump of Czechoslovakia, it gained not only the important Skoda and CKD/Praga arms manufacturing works but also large numbers of capable Czechoslovak tanks including the CKD/Praga TNHP (LT-38) light tank that was pressed into German service as the PzKpfw 38(t), which remained in production up to 1942 and was used by several Panzer divisions created in the early part of World War II.*

Yugoslavia's adherence to the Axis agreement was repudiated. The German 2nd Army, with the 1st Panzergruppe and XLVI Panzer Corps under command, was instrumental in the conquest of Yugoslavia with the support of the Italian 2nd Army and Hungarian 3rd Army, while the German 12th Army, with the XL Panzer Corps under command, was similarly instrumental in the conquest of Greece with the support of the Italian 9th and 11th Armies.

This diversion was costly not only in terms of men and matériel, but more importantly in terms of time as it pushed the launch of 'Barbarossa', the invasion of the western USSR, back to 21 June 1941.

*Fixed fortifications, such as those exemplified here in this cutaway illustration, featured strongly in the defensive plans of many nations during the 1920s and 1930s, but despite their enormous cost and carefully planned construction proved to be relatively ineffective even when they could not be outflanked and were therefore attacked frontally.*

Despite this fact, the invasion seemed at first to be proceeding with enormous success. The German armies were tough, fit, well trained and now highly experienced in the tactical and operational aspects of *Blitzkrieg* warfare, and the four Panzergruppen that spearheaded the offensive were among the finest troops in the world at that time, with large numbers of battle-proved fighting vehicles. The advance of Generalfeldmarschall Wilhelm Ritter von Leeb's Army Group 'North' towards Leningrad was led by Generaloberst Erich Hoepner's 4th Panzergruppe (three Panzer and three infantry divisions) and the advance of Generalfeldmarschall Gerd von Rundstedt's Army Group 'South' into the Ukraine was led by Generaloberst Ewald von Kleist's 1st Panzergruppe (five Panzer and three infantry divisions), while the primary central thrust towards Moscow by Generalfeldmarschall Fedor von Bock's Army Group 'Centre' was based on the deep penetrations and pincer envelopments of two Panzergruppen, namely Generaloberst Hermann Hoth's 3rd Panzergruppe (four Panzer and three infantry divisions) in the north and Generaloberst Heinz Guderian's 2nd Panzergruppe (five Panzer and four infantry divisions) in the south.

The German offensive was therefore undertaken by 17 Panzer divisions and 103 German infantry divisions supported in the south by 14 Rumanian

*The fog of war: German infantry move forward through a destroyed barbed-wire entanglement.*

and two Hungarian infantry divisions, and in the extreme north by a 15-division Finnish offensive itself supported by five German divisions.

On the other side of the front, the Soviets had 28 tank divisions, but this notional superiority in armoured strength was not in any sense a real superiority. The Soviet tank divisions were not grouped in homogeneous formations resembling the German Panzergruppen, but instead were allocated to each of the armies that the Soviet high command had positioned close to the frontier but with no strength in depth. Lacking the same level of combat experience as their German opponents and relying on a tactical mix of infantry and tank formations that had been rendered obsolete by the German concept of *Blitzkrieg* warfare, the Soviet armies were completely outmatched by the German forces, especially as the Panzergruppen were always able to achieve a local superiority of armoured force against Soviet forces whose tank strength was less capable than that of the Germans.

The result was a series of fast, deep penetrations by the Germans, and these advances yielded vast numbers of Soviet prisoners and huge gains of matériel. The Germans continued their progress ever deeper into western Russia, but the distances involved were huge and the Germans' transport resources were limited, with the result that the pace of the advance slowed

*German infantry were notably adept at the tactic of forward rushing under the cover of artillery or mortar fire.*

**Opposite top:** *The movement of super-heavy artillery by rail was a good idea in theory, but the Germans found that in practice there was often little for these large and very expensive equipments to tackle, except in unusual circumstances such as the German siege of Sevastopol in the summer of 1942.*

**Opposite bottom:** *The weapon most strongly associated with the German effort in World War II remains the class '88', a piece of 88mm (3.465in) artillery designed for anti-aircraft use but also superb in the anti-tank role.*

steadily as men and horses became exhausted, and the Soviets' scorched-earth policy made it increasingly difficult for the Germans to use the remnants of the Soviet road and rail networks to bring up the fuel and ammunition supplies required to sustain the momentum of the advance by the Panzer and motorised forces.

The pace of the German advance was then slowed further by the advent of the autumn rains, which turned virtually every surviving road and most of the countryside into thick, sticking mud. Then came the winter, and with this the autumn mud froze and the temperature plummeted, virtually immobilising the German forces that lacked even the most basic of winter equipment for their vehicles and personnel. The advance of Army Group 'Centre' reached the very outskirts of Moscow before being halted, but then the primary German objective was pushed out of reach by the arrival from Siberia of fresh Soviet forces familiar with the bitter conditions and well equipped to survive them. With the arrival of these Siberian forces, Germany's last chance of a quick and decisive victory over the USSR disappeared.

Did this opportunity for victory in 1941 ever exist? According to the German generals it did, and the only factors preventing the capture of Moscow were the delay imposed by the onset of autumn and winter weather, and the constant interference of Hitler in operational matters. Yet this is a simplistic view that fails to take into account the determined resistance of the Soviet forces and people, who would have fought on even if Moscow had fallen: essential equipment of all types had been removed or destroyed before the Germans arrived, and whole industrial complexes had been uprooted and transported to safe areas east of the Ural mountains for extraordinarily rapid re-establishment and resumption of production.

More significantly, there was a major fault in the design for 'Barbarossa':

*Seen here in front three-quarter and cutaway forms, the PzKpfw VI Tiger II heavy tank was arguably the finest armoured fighting vehicle of its type to appear in World War II, and was otherwise known as the Königstiger (King Tiger, sometimes rendered Royal Tiger). The type was very heavily armoured and was armed with a potent 88mm (3.465in) high-velocity gun, but was tactically hampered by its weight and, perhaps more significantly, its poor power-to-weight ratio.*

*Super-heavy rail guns could fire heavy shells to a considerable range with great accuracy, but were expensive to manufacture and also required very large crews including security troops, administrative troops, railway troops, cooks etc. under the command of a senior officer.*

this was the incomprehensible German failure to take the very size of the USSR into realistic account. The vastness of the country rendered *Blitzkrieg* warfare pointless except at the operational level and below, and the huge numbers of Soviet military personnel made it impossible for the Luftwaffe to disrupt the Soviet rear areas and thus prevent the arrival of fresh troops and equipment. As well as exhausting men and horses, the distances involved also caused considerable mechanical wear in all types of vehicles, and this was exacerbated by the dust of the region: the result was that motor vehicles and tanks needed considerably more maintenance than had been anticipated. With the exception of the highway between Minsk and Moscow, there were few metalled roads in western Russia, and motor vehicles became bogged down once these non-metalled roads turned to deep mud with the onset of the autumn rains. Finally, the Soviet railway gauge was different from that used by the Germans, and as the retreating Soviets had removed or destroyed all rolling stock, the Germans had to alter all the railways to the German gauge before they could run their own rolling stock on them.

All these factors contributed in great measure to the increasing exhaustion of the German forces the farther to the east they moved, and this tendency was worsened by the fact that, after launching their offensive over a large front extending from the Black Sea in the south to the Baltic Sea in the north, they were moving into an even wider tract of territory with Army Group 'North' moving north-east towards Leningrad, Army Group 'Centre' moving east towards Moscow, and Army Group 'South' moving south-east towards

The fact that infantry support and anti-tank guns often had to operate within rifle or machine gun range of their targets meant that such equipments were almost universally fitted with a shield to protect the crew against such fire as well as shell fragments.

Lines of concrete 'dragon's teeth' were much used by the Germans in an effort to provide anti-tank defences across the main lines of advance into Germany. The concept was that any tank attempting to climb and cross such defence lines would probably lose a track or, alternatively, expose its lightly armoured belly to anti-tank fire as it climbed the first line of teeth.

*With Reichsführer-SS Heinrich Himmler watching in the background (far right), Hitler receives a briefing from senior commanders in the field. German operations right down to the tactical levels were frequently subjected to Hitler's interference even when he was nowhere near the front.*

Kiev and the Ukraine. This meant that the three axes of advance were diverging from each other, and the deeper the Germans moved into Russia the further apart their three main groupings became: this made it increasingly difficult for the Germans to concentrate their forces in an emergency, and correspondingly easier for the Soviets to achieve local superiority of force in their efforts to check the pace and distance of the German advances.

Added to the fact that the German forces were operating in what might be described as a territorial vacuum containing large numbers of Soviet forces but no decisive strategic objectives, they were also operating in a strategic vacuum for the high command had failed to fix any real strategic objective other than the destruction of the Soviet state and the political system it controlled. The only final geographical objective ever mooted was the ill-defined line between Astrakhan in the south on the Caspian Sea and Archangel in the north on the White Sea, but while this line might have looked impressive on the map it offered no features that would have allowed the Germans to create an effective defence line.

Another problem facing the German campaign was the ever-increasing length of the front as the German armies pushed forward. The fluidity of the operational situation therefore placed great emphasis on the need for precise and timely orders from the high command in reflection of the changing front

*Heinz Guderian may rightly be called the father of the Panzer force, and was one of the ablest German operational commanders of World War II.*

*The Sturmmörser Tiger, of which a mere 10 were completed as PzKpfw VI Tiger Ausf E conversions, was an assault weapon with the turret adapted for the carriage of a 380mm (14.96in) launcher for rockets whose exhaust gases were turned through 180° to be vented forward via the ring of small tubes in the wall of the dumpy rocket-launcher 'barrel'.*

line situation, and also on the need for fraternal co-operation between army group and army commanders. Neither of these needs was satisfied during 'Barbarossa'. Orders from the top were bedevilled by Hitler's constant meddling, always on the grounds of what he believed should be happening rather than what was actually happening, and the inability of the OKH to formulate any order that was both practical and timely. At the front, the chance of fraternal co-operation was rendered virtually impossible by diversions of concentration and by rivalries.

*German infantrymen have to unload a truck that has fallen through a make-shift bridge.*

Von Bock, for example, wanted to be remembered in history as the first man after Napoleon to have captured Moscow, but instead of concentrating on this single and monumentally difficult task, he allowed himself to be diverted constantly by the efforts of subordinates who supported the growing resistance to Hitler and who plagued their commander-in-chief with requests to take the lead in organising an army coup against the Führer. Further down the chain of command in Army Group 'Centre' were rivals such as Ewald von Kleist and Heinz Guderian, commanding the 4th Army and 2nd Panzergruppe respectively. Von Kleist, who had commanded the Panzer force in the invasion of France, now complained unceasingly that Guderian led his Panzer force off into the distance without regard for his infantry army, which was therefore left without armoured support, while Guderian was constantly annoyed by any orders to check the rate of his advance and generally ignored them.

The situation was worsened by the increasing command impotence of the two officers heading the OKH, namely Generalfeldmarschall von Brauchitsch and Generaloberst Franz Halder. By the time of the start of 'Barbarossa' in June 1941, both these senior officers knew that they were to play the role of implementing the demands of Hitler's 'intuitive' strategic genius rather than themselves controlling the course of the campaign. The effect of this tendency is nowhere better exemplified than in the waste of some two and a half weeks in the decision as to whether the Ukraine or

The Germans achieved considerable military feats in North Africa when they had adequate equipment and enough fuel, but the provision of these across the British-dominated central sector of the Mediterranean was always difficult.

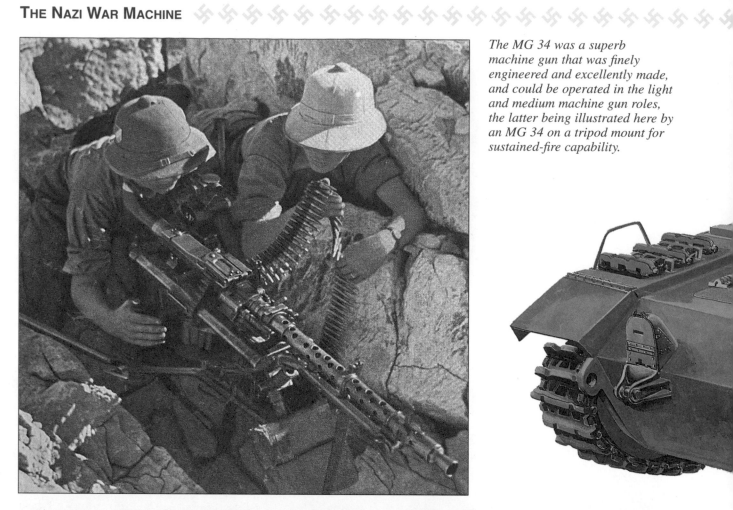

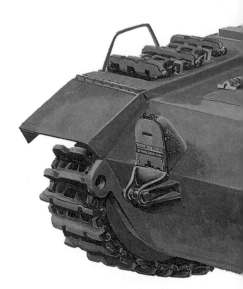

*The MG 34 was a superb machine gun that was finely engineered and excellently made, and could be operated in the light and medium machine gun roles, the latter being illustrated here by an MG 34 on a tripod mount for sustained-fire capability.*

*The Sturmgeschütz III was an assault gun conversion of the obsolete PzKpfw III medium tank, the traversing turret being replaced by a fixed barbette carrying a 75mm (2.95in) short-barrel gun on a limited-traverse mounting.*

***Opposite below:*** *A feature of most German artillery, such as this equipment camouflaged with debris in an effort to avoid Allied air attack, was the use of solid rather than pneumatic rubber tyres.*

Moscow was to be the primary objective of the campaign's first stage. The army felt that Moscow should be its primary objective, and the task of persuading the Führer of this fact at a high command meeting at Lötzen on 23 August was entrusted to Guderian by Halder and Bock, neither of whom had the nerve to tackle Hitler directly. Then von Brauchitsch learned of this fact and ordered Guderian not even to mention Moscow to Hitler, but Guderian decided that it was necessary and suggested that the Soviet capital was more important than the Ukraine. None of the other generals present now supported Guderian, who was left isolated as his fellow generals concurred with Hitler's demand that the Ukraine should be cleared first, as it was of more economic importance to Germany.

This decision cost some two and a half weeks of vital campaigning time, with the result that the German forces were only on the outskirts of Moscow when winter and the Siberian reinforcements arrived. Germany's chance, if chance it was, had been lost to the error of Hitler's strategic vision and the sycophancy of Germany's most senior generals. To add insult to the injury already being suffered by the German forces in the field, the advent of winter found them totally without adequate winter clothing, such stocks as there were having been stranded in Warsaw as a result of dreadful inefficiency in the quartermaster department.

Hitler's response to the failure before Moscow in December 1941 was the wholesale dismissal of many senior commanders and, more importantly, the personal assumption of the role of army commander-in-chief as successor to von Brauchitsch. Having failed to find a way to check Hitler's intuition with professional counsel, the army high command now found its role usurped by a man whose concept of strategy embodied an increasing insistence on standing fast under any and all situations. This policy was often ignored by front-line commanders, to their considerable peril when the fact was discovered by Hitler, but inevitably exacted an intolerably high price on Germany's capabilities on the Eastern Front: armies were forced to create defences in the wrong places, and as well as costing the Germans vast quantities of irreplaceable manpower and matériel, this also offered considerable strategic opportunities to the increasingly capable Soviet high command.

As the German invasion of the USSR was creating the situation that led inevitably to Germany's final defeat, the only other purely military theatre in which German forces were playing an active part was North Africa. The

Italian forces of Benito Mussolini's Fascist regime had sought to expel the British from Egypt with an offensive from Cyrenaica, the eastern part of the Italian colony of Libya. The effort had been an abject failure that turned to disaster as the British, despite their complete numerical inferiority to the Italian total of 250,000 men in nine regular, three 'Blackshirt' and two native divisions, checked the advance of Mareschale Graziani's force and then, with only 36,000 men, went over to an offensive that drove the Italians out of Cyrenaica into Tripolitania, and in the process captured very large numbers of Italians.

Asked by Mussolini for support, Hitler responded with the offer of limited forces under a capable German commander, General Erwin Rommel, who had distinguished himself as commander of the 7th Panzer Division in the French campaign. With 'Barbarossa' looming, the German force readied for despatch to North Africa in February 1941 comprised the 5th Light and 15th Panzer Divisions, neither of which would be up to full strength until May, when the Germans were scheduled to begin operations. Rommel was not the commander to wait when he saw an opportunity for offensive action, however, and he launched an immediate offensive that expelled the British from Cyrenaica back into Egypt. This was a considerable achievement, but caught the OKW and OKH completely off balance as it opened the possibility of further operations at a time when Rommel's forces could not be reinforced.

The result was a see-saw campaign in which the front line moved east and west along the North African shore as each side was able to secure a superiority in manpower, weapons and, most importantly of all, fuel. Rommel became a thorn in the British side for his apparent ability not only to recover from reverses but to turn such reverses into the springboards for successful offensive action. It was only in the summer of 1942 that Hitler finally decided that North Africa was a theatre in which Germany could score

*Opposite, top and bottom: Winter operations on the Eastern Front caused the Germans enormous problems as they lacked the experience of and equipment for such conditions in the face of an enemy which was able to survive and operate effectively in them.*

*The European and western Russian railway systems constituted some of the main arteries of supply for the German forces, but were often unavailable for specific military tasks such as requirement for the movement of large numbers to concentration and extermination camps or, later in the war, for the evacuation of civilians in the face of Allied and Soviet advances.*

*The FlaK 30 was a 20mm anti-aircraft gun that was towed on a two-wheel carriage whose wheels were removed as the equipment was emplaced for action. The FlaK 30 was built in large numbers and remained in service right through World War II.*

a strategically important success, but this decision came too late for the small German force that was decisively defeated, together with its Italian allies, after attempting a final invasion of Egypt. The Axis effort was checked in July 1942, and in November the revitalised British 8th Army broke the Panzerarmee Afrika in the 2nd Battle of El Alamein. In the same month American and British forces landed on the other side of the continent in French Morocco and Algeria, and the westward and eastward advances of the two groups of Allied forces soon trapped the German and Italian forces, now somewhat too grandly named Army Group 'Africa', in Tunisia where its remnants were driven to defeat in May 1943.

Rommel escaped from this disaster as he had recently returned to Germany as a sick man, but some 250,000 experienced soldiers plus all their equipment and weapons were lost. The fault for this failure must lie entirely with Hitler and the army high command, for they allowed themselves to be persuaded by Rommel's successes in 1941 and the first part of 1942 to raise the theatre from one of secondary to primary importance. As a theatre now deemed to be of primary importance, North Africa should therefore have received the men, weapons and equipment it required: the fact that the Allies had virtually total command of the sea and could prevent the delivery of these reinforcements should have made the German high command think again about the raising of North Africa to primary status.

By April 1942 the Germans had checked the Soviet offensive that had started around Moscow in December 1941, and in January 1942 checked an offensive south of Kharkov before throwing it back and seizing more territory in May. This paved the way for the Germans' summer offensive of 1942, which was an enormous undertaking designed to sweep south-east through the 'Donets corridor' so that von Bock's Army Group 'B' could then attack east to take Stalingrad on the River Volga as Generalfeldmarschall Wilhelm List's new Army Group 'A' struck farther to the south-east across the lower reaches of the Rivers Don and Donets to plunge into the Caucasus with the object of taking the oilfields at Maykop, Grozny and Baku. All went well at first, but Generaloberst Friedrich Paulus's 6th Army and part of Generaloberst Hermann Hoth's 4th Panzerarmee were checked after taking only part of Stalingrad, and Army Group 'A' was checked well short of its final objectives in the Caucasus region.

There were three reasons for this failure. The first of these was the growing Soviet sophistication in tactical and operational matters, which persuaded them to fall back rather than risk encirclement followed by destruction or surrender: the effect of this change was not only to preserve Soviet lives, but also to allow the dissemination of hard-won tactical experience through the formations of the Soviet army. The second reason was Hitler's increasingly unreliable strategic reasoning, which

*This cutaway illustration of the Sturmgeschütz III reveals the significant reduction in height and vulnerability that was achieved by the replacement of the traversing turret of the PzKpfw III baseline vehicle by this assault gun conversion's fixed barbette.*

*PzKpfw 35(t) was the German designation for a Czechoslovak light tank, the Skoda S-IIa (LT-35) of which considerable numbers were seized in 1939 and pressed into service with the Panzer divisions.*

demanded outright offensives wherever possible but then reduced their overall efficiency by allocating too many objectives and thereby diluting the strength available to each objective. The summer offensive of 1942 was a case in point, for Hitler wanted both Stalingrad and the oilfields of the Caucasus, and this meant that the 4th Panzerarmee was used first to help secure the crossings of the River Don for the Caucasus part of the campaign, and then pulled back for use in the Stalingrad operation: the resultant delay was fatal, for the Germans lost the chance to seize Stalingrad against limited resistance in August and therefore persuaded Paulus, in his first independent command, to undertake a tactically futile head-on assault against much strengthened Soviet defences. The third reason was Hitler's obdurate insistence that ground captured with German blood should not be yielded: at the time of its encirclement in Stalingrad, the 6th Army could probably have broken out without undue difficulty, but Paulus adhered to Hitler's orders and stood fast. It is worth noting, however, that Hitler and Paulus were not alone in believing that the Germans could hold the city and beat off the Soviet assaults, for early in the war large pockets of German troops at Demyansk and Kholm had achieved just this with the aid of the Luftwaffe's transport capability.

The scene was now set for a truly disastrous episode in the history of German arms. The Soviets pounced on the isolated German position in Stalingrad, and in November 1942 launched a huge pincer movement that in four days swept through the flanking defences of the Rumanian 3rd and 4th Armies to trap the 6th Army and part of the 4th Panzerarmee in Stalingrad. The rest of the 4th Panzerarmee launched a major effort to relieve the forces in Stalingrad during December, but was checked well short of the city (whose German garrison, Hitler had been assured by Reichsmarschall Hermann Goering, was in no danger as it could easily be supplied with all necessary food, ammunition, fuel and other equipment by his Luftwaffe). In fact, the Luftwaffe never managed to achieve the required daily rate of deliveries, and as the Soviets tightened their noose round the beleaguered garrison, both the airfields were lost to the Germans, whose last 200,000 men were finally starved into surrender in February 1943 after 100,000 more had been killed in the fighting and only 34,000 were evacuated by air.

The loss of the 6th Army deprived the German army on the Eastern Front of its single most capable field force, and the lowering of morale that followed the defeat at Stalingrad was reinforced only four months later by the loss of Army Group 'Africa'. With these twin losses it should have been clear to all in Germany that the war was lost.

The tide was now definitely running in favour of the Soviets, who quickly regained all the territory they had lost earlier in the year and were then checked only by the tactical genius of Generalfeldmarschall Erich von Manstein in command of Army Group 'Don'. Von Manstein's success pushed the Soviets back in the region around Kharkov and farther to the south, leaving the Soviets with a large salient centred on Kursk. This was the spot selected by Hitler for a third German summer offensive: it was known that the Soviets had reinforced the Kursk salient to a formidable degree (the Germans did not know actually how formidable the Soviet defences were), but Hitler was convinced that the salient could be pinched off by attacks on its shoulders, thereby restoring the strategic initiative on the Eastern Front to the German army.

The undertaking was entrusted to Generaloberst Walter Model's 9th Army of Generalfeldmarschall Walter von Kluge's Army Group 'Centre', which was to attack south-east from a point south of Orel, and to Generaloberst

Hermann Hoth's 4th Panzerarmee and General Wilhelm Kempf's Operational Group 'Kempf' of Generalfeldmarschall Erich von Manstein's Army Group 'South', which were to attack north-east from a point north of Kharkov, the object being the junction of the two armies to the east of Kursk, thereby cutting off the two Soviet fronts (army groups) holding the perimeter of the salient.

Under the less than enthusiastic supervision of Generaloberst Heinz Guderian, now inspector of armoured forces and a firm believer that the new tanks should not be committed to battle until large numbers were available to ensure the destruction of the Soviets' T-34 tank force, the Panzer divisions earmarked for the offensive were refitted as far as was possible with the new PzKpfw V Panther medium tanks and PzKpfw VI Tiger heavy tanks.

The offensive was launched on 4 July 1943, and was a complete disaster for Germany. Warned of the German build-up and plans, by local reconnaissance and agents, the Soviets were waiting for the Germans in massively entrenched positions established in great depth and with a full

front in reserve. The Germans did make limited progress in the north and south, but by 10 July had been shattered by the Soviets' magnificent combination of determination, artillery, tanks and air power. The 9th Army gained 6 miles (9.65km) at the cost of 25,000 dead as well as 200 tanks and 200 aircraft destroyed, while the 4th Panzerarmee and the Operational Group 'Kempf' were able to advance 25 miles (40km) at the cost of 10,000 men and 350 tanks in a vast tank battle that raged in the area around Pokrovka.

Shattered by the effects of their own offensive, the German forces could not resist the counter-offensive that the Russians immediately launched to eliminate the German salients around Orel and Kharkov. In August the rest of the Soviet armies went over to the offensive between a point north-west of Moscow and the Sea of Azov, driving the Germans back along the southern three-quarters of the Eastern Front.

Just after the start of the Germans' 'Zitadelle' (citadel) offensive at Kursk, the Allies landed in Sicily at the beginning of a campaign desired by the British rather than the Americans as a means of striking at the 'soft underbelly' of the Axis powers. With the Kursk operation in full swing, and indeed beginning to falter, there was nothing that the Germans could do to reinforce Italy, where Generalfeldmarschall Albert Kesselring co-ordinated the defence. The defence of Sicily was left to the Italians, reinforced by two German divisions, while Kesselring concentrated on the Allies' inevitable next move, an invasion of Italy itself.

Anticipating the probability of an Italian armistice with the Allies, which came into effect on 9 September, the Germans had laid plans for an

Large, weighty, possessing a poor power-to-weight ratio, and fitted with thick vertical rather than more effective inclined but thinner armour, the PzKpfw VI Tiger was very powerfully armed and offered considerable capabilities in purely defensive fighting, placing little demand on mobility.

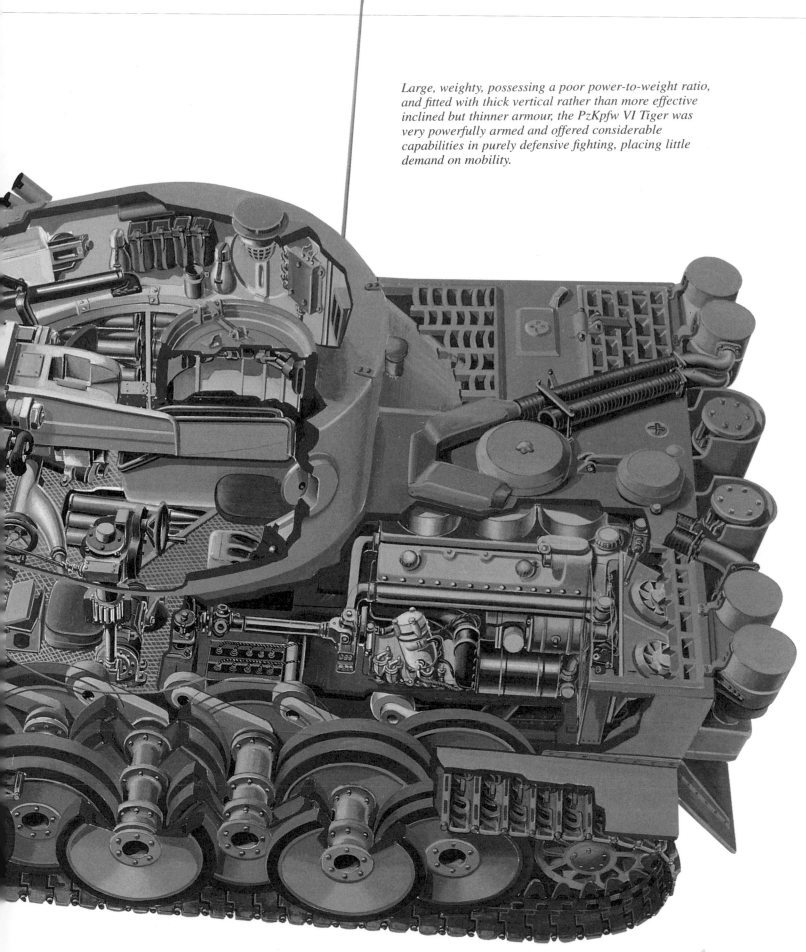

*The quality of German commissioned and non-commissioned officers, most of them experienced after long careers in the Reichsheer, was very high in the early stages of World War II.*

occupation of Italy and the implementation of these plans little affected the German reply to the Allied landing at Salerno in the Bay of Naples on 9 September. There followed a bitter and extremely costly 21-month campaign as the Allies drove north along the Italian peninsula with the Americans mainly on the western side and the British on the eastern side. Kesselring proved himself a genius at defensive warfare, using the natural features of the Apennine mountains, and in particular the deep valleys, to create defensive positions of enormous strength. Fighting against these defensive positions cost the Allies time, lives and matériel, and in this defensive war Kesselring was very ably supported by the commanders of his two subordinate armies, namely Generaloberst Heinrich von Vietinghoff-Scheel of the 10th Army and Generaloberst Eberhard von Mackensen of the 14th Army. As the Allied offensives approached northern Italy, Kesselring was shifted to a more important position against the Allies in north-west Europe, von Vietinghoff-Scheel assuming command of Army Group 'C' with the 10th and 14th Armies now commanded by General Traugott Herr and General Joachim Lemelsen respectively.

More than any other campaign, however, the war in Italy revealed the particular virtues of the German army as a fighting machine capable of sustained operations, often under the command of relatively junior officers, and under the most adverse of conditions (in this case almost total Allied air superiority). The nature of the war in Italy dictated relatively small-scale battles fought by divisions as much as corps, and here the training and initiative of the middle-rank commanders, who had learned their skills in the Reichsheer of the inter-war years, made their units and formations notably skilful enemies for the Allies. The Germans were beaten, and finally beaten decisively, but their defensive campaign was still full of lessons in the art of defensive warfare.

On the Eastern Front, the summer of 1943 should have been used for the creation of a powerful German fall-back position along the line of the River Dniepr, which could have been made strong enough to constitute a formidable barrier to further Soviet advances until the spring of 1944, thereby buying time for the German forces on the Eastern Front to be revived by rest and re-equipment as they were rotated out of the shorter and more defensible line offered by the Dniepr. Hitler would not entertain this notion because of his obsession with not yielding ground, and the result was

*A German infantryman advances under fire on the Eastern Front, his weapon being the standard 7.92mm (0.312in) Gewehr 98k bolt-action rifle.*

inevitable: through the summer, autumn and early winter of 1943 the Soviet armies careered forward in a fashion which the Germans were powerless to counter. Constantly the Germans hoped that a river barrier might at least slow the Soviets, but constantly they found that the creation of even a small Soviet bridgehead was immediately followed by a flood of Soviet infantry, armour and artillery. The Germans were thus driven back without any possibility of pulling back on their own terms, and it was November 1943 before the Soviets finally called a temporary halt.

By this time the Germans were faced with the imminence of a third front in north-west Europe to complement the Eastern and Italian Fronts. It was clear that the long-expected American and British amphibious assault on the German positions in France would not long be delayed, and considerable thought was therefore given to the task of fighting a three-front war. Curiously, the officer who offered the most daring and realistic plan for Germany's longer-term survival, was the essentially timorous Jodl, the OKW chief-of-staff. Jodl's plan was for the German armies on the Eastern Front to disengage and fall back to Germany's eastern frontier, which was shorter in length than the current front and could therefore be held more strongly with a smaller number of divisions, freeing the others for service on what would become the Western Front after the Allies had landed in France.

This suggestion was anathema to Hitler, and the German armies on the Eastern Front were condemned to a continuing campaign with the Soviets, who launched their Belorussian offensive in June 1944 to balance the gains made in the Ukraine at the end of the previous year.

*Opposite: Seen here in the direct-fire role, German heavy artillery was generally of excellent quality and was always handled efficiently for the tactical support of the ground forces.*

Lasting to the end of August 1944, the Belorussian campaign took the Soviets into central Poland and effectively destroyed Army Group 'Centre', which during this period had a succession of three commanders in the form of Generalfeldmarschall Ernst Busch, Generalfeldmarschall Walter Model and Generaloberst Georg-Hans Reinhardt. Further to the north, the Soviets also entered the Baltic states, where the hapless Army Group 'North' also underwent two changes of command as Generaloberst Georg Lindemann was replaced by Generaloberst Johannes Friessner and he in turn by Generaloberst Ferdinand Schörner.

By the time the Belorussian offensive's success had begun to sink into the minds of the German high command, the Americans and British had landed in Normandy to open a third front. This spurred the efforts of a small number of middle-ranking officers to murder Hitler, after which they believed the Allies would be willing to negotiate with a more level-headed German regime. The 'bomb plot' of July 1944 failed to kill Hitler, but the assassination attempt by German officers so outraged many senior German officers that some of them, including Guderian, were willing to sit in judgement on the plotters.

The German army was now being squeezed steadily by a vice with three jaws. With one of those ironies so much loved by history, however, never had the German army been better equipped than at this moment of crisis:

*For its time, the PzKpfw III was a good medium tank well suited to mobile operations on large battlefields, but was hampered in longer-term development by the small size of its turret ring, which prevented the installation of a significantly larger-calibre gun with the type of long barrel needed for the generation of the high muzzle velocity required to give the projectile good armour-penetration qualities.*

Germany was now belatedly on a total war footing, and under the energetic and highly capable supervision of Albert Speer, the minister of armaments, German factories were delivering large numbers of advanced weapons including the Panther and Tiger tanks that were relatively immune to the attentions of all Allied tanks but the Soviet IS series of heavy tanks and the Sherman 'Firefly' (the ubiquitous American Sherman medium tank regunned with a British 17pdr anti-tank gun). Other important German weapons of this period included the Nebelwerfer artillery rocket launcher that could lay down enormously potent barrages of fire at considerably less production cost than artillery, and the Panzerfaust and Panzerschreck anti-tank rocket launchers. These and other weapons were being produced in prodigious numbers, but it was too late for the German army even if its own leaders refused to accept the fact: there was now just too much opposition, strong not only in numbers but also in determination, fighting skills and weapons, and at last the Allied strategic bombing campaign was beginning to exert a real effect as its efforts cut Germany's lines of communication and started to destroy its production of energy, especially synthetic oil products.

In the summer and autumn of 1944, the major Soviet and Allied armies surged forward from east and west respectively, halting finally only as a result of exhaustion of men and consumables (ammunition and fuel) rather than German action. This condemned Europe to another winter of warfare before the matter could finally be resolved in 1945.

From west and east the Allies and the Soviets were now faced with the monumentally difficult task of fighting their way deep into Germany and crushing all resistance. This was an undertaking thought not to be insuperable in purely military terms, for the Germans were already beaten

*German infantry, the nearer man carrying an MG 34 machine gun in its bipod-fitted light machine gun form, move up toward the enemy in the lee of a German tank.*

*A piece of German heavy artillery is seen in action on the Eastern Front, where the numbers and capabilities of the German artillery arm were overshadowed by the equal skills and superior numbers of the Soviets' artillery arm.*

even though they would not admit the fact, but reckoned to be dangerous in terms of the numbers of Soviet and Allied casualties. The Soviets and Allies therefore steeled themselves for a bloody termination to the war, but once again Hitler played into their hands and helped reduce the duration and capability of the German resistance.

Throughout the autumn and early winter of 1945 Germany had been husbanding its strength, building up its armoured reserves and creating a small stockpile of fuel for the defence of the Reich. Hitler had other ideas, however, and ordered that this limited strength be used in a major offensive designed to cut the Allied armies into two groups as the German forces smashed their way west out of the Ardennes once more, seized Allied fuel dumps and then wheeled north-west to take the Belgian port of Antwerp, recently established as the Allies' main forward-supply port. This, Hitler believed, would revive German fortunes and, with large quantities of captured fuel at their disposal, the German armies would then destroy the Canadian 1st, British 2nd and US 9th and 1st Armies trapped in northern Belgium and the southern Netherlands, and then turn south to destroy the other Allied armies before recapturing western Europe.

The formation entrusted with this fanciful scenario was Generalfeldmarschall Walter Model's Army Group 'B', whose main constituents from north to south were SS Oberstgruppenführer Josef 'Sepp' Dietrich's 6th SS Panzerarmee, General Hasso von Manteuffel's 5th Panzerarmee and General Erich Brandenberger's 7th Army with a total of 7½ Panzer Divisions between them. In theory, this was a formidable force that represented a real threat to the Allies, especially as these divisions had large numbers of modern tanks. The tanks were desperately short of fuel, however, and were manned by men who generally lacked the experience and maturity of their predecessors in the tank arm. The same was also true of the accompanying infantry, which included large numbers of older men, and adolescents who lacked both the training and combat experience of their predecessors.

Accustomed to seeing what he wanted to see rather than realistic fact, Hitler therefore believed that he had a powerful force at his disposal. The offensive began on 15 December 1944, and initially achieved a significant breakthrough as this sector of the front was held only in light strength by American formations resting from the rigours of the previous battles. The German forces poured through the breach in the American line and headed for Dinant on the River Meuse, in the process creating a large salient, or bulge, after which the battle received its popular nickname 'Battle of the Bulge'.

The fate of Army Group 'B' was sealed by its failure to capture the required fuel and the stubborn resistance of the US 101st airborne division at Bastogne, which slowed the German advance and provided time for the Allies to bolster their positions on the shoulders of the German breakthrough and start moving forces to contain the breakthrough itself. This would have been sufficient to defeat the German offensive, but then the arrival of better weather allowed the resumption of Allied tactical air operations to crush the last efforts of the crumbling offensive. By the beginning of January 1945 the Germans had lost two-thirds of the ground they had recaptured, and by the end of the first week in February they had been driven back to their start line.

The 'Battle of the Bulge' wasted Germany's last significant reserve, which was almost immediately needed for Germany's now impossible task of stemming the wide-front offensive that the Soviets launched in the east on 11 January. The Soviets erupted from their lodgement west of the River Vistula around Warsaw and smashed their way forward to the west, reaching the line of the River Oder, little short of Berlin, by the beginning of February. At this time the Allies were still battling their way forward through the 'Siegfried Line', towards their objectives in the west.

Yet again, Hitler's obsessions played a major part in facilitating the further advances of the Soviets and the Allies. These two factors were his insistence on keeping Hungary in the war by bolstering its declining military capability with German formations that could have been far better employed in the defence of the Reich, and his increasing preoccupation with 'fortress' defence. The latter concept meant that every significant town was declared a fortress that could not be yielded to the Soviets, and this required additional troops to be sent to these places, which were often of little tactical or operational significance and were lost as the Soviets completed their encirclements of the fortress areas and pounded them to destruction with artillery. Perhaps the most wasteful of all these fortress areas was the Kurland peninsula on the southern side of the Gulf of Riga, where 18 divisions of Army Group 'Kurland' were wasted even though they could have been evacuated by sea had Hitler approved.

The final defeat of Germany began in March 1945, when the Allies managed to cross the River Rhine (Germany's main natural defence in the west) and poured through to the east, in the process surrounding the Ruhr industrial region that was absolutely essential to the continued survival of Germany's military capability. Trapped in the Ruhr pocket were Model together with the 5th Panzerarmee and 15th Army, which eventually yielded 317,000 prisoners of war. The remnants of three German army groups continued to resist in the west, but by the middle of April the British and Canadians in the north, the Americans in the centre, and the Americans and French in the south had swept forward all along the front to reach a line about 75 miles (120km) from Berlin at its closest point.

*Opposite: The speed and overwhelming success of the Germans' deep-penetration tactics in the first part of World War II resulted in comparatively little of what is now termed 'collateral damage', but the slogging of the later campaigns, as the Germans fought with dogged bitterness to avoid being pushed back from their gains earlier in the war, resulted in far higher levels of damage including almost total destruction of certain parts of Germany.*

On the other side of the German capital, Army Groups 'Vistula' and 'Centre', under the command of Generaloberste Gotthard Heinrici and Ferdinand Schörner respectively, managed to check the final Soviet advance on Berlin for short periods, but were gradually driven back by a Soviet superiority of two-to-one in men and aircraft and four-to-one in tanks and artillery. The Soviets swept round Berlin, which was isolated from the rest of Germany on 15 April, and the last stages of the war in Europe began. Hitler committed suicide on 30 April, and on 2 May the Soviets completed their virtually total destruction of Berlin with tanks and artillery.

The Soviets and Allies met along the line of the River Elbe from 18 April, and on 7 May the last Germans forces surrendered unconditionally.

# DIE KRIEGSMARINE

The Kriegsmarine, or navy, was by far the weakest of the German armed force in World War II, yet it had to face a generally stronger enemy throughout the war in a fashion that the army and air force only came to appreciate from 1943 onwards. This weakness of strength was compounded by Germany's poor naval location with coastlines only on the southern sides of the North Sea and Baltic Sea, which gave the navy an essentially impossible task in seeking to gain command of the seas from its home bases. The entry of Italy into the war in June 1940 opened the way for the basing of German ships in the Mediterranean, although they had to run the British gauntlet in the Strait of Gibraltar. Rumania's entry into the war in June 1941 added bases on the western side of the Black Sea, and successes of the army's campaigns between 1939 and the end of 1941 provided additional ports between France's frontier with Spain and the Gulf of Finland with a northern extension along the coast of Norway up to the North Cape.

Despite the extension of its bases, the navy soon found that it could not successfully operate large surface vessels in the face of overwhelming British and subsequent American strength despite the isolated successes of elements such as its surface raiders in the first two years of the war, which had enjoyed the advantages of a reduced numerical inferiority *vis-à-vis* its opponents.

The decline of the German navy's surface capability was more than counterbalanced by the growth of its submarine arm, which from 1940 gradually assumed a dominant role in naval affairs and also became one of Germany's main hopes of securing eventual victory over the British by cutting the maritime links by which food, fuel, raw materials and weapons reached British ports. This 'Battle of the Atlantic' reached its grim climax in mid-1943 after building steadily during 1941 and 1942, but the Germans found that skill and courage were not sufficient to beat the Allies' skill and courage in combination with greater production capability and an increasingly decisive edge in the technological battle.

The genesis of the Kriegsmarine can be found in November 1918, a mere 10 days after the end of World War I, when the German High Seas Fleet

The German submarine arm was considerably more successful than its surface arm counterpart in World War II, but the exigencies of the situation late in the war led to the construction of large numbers of small and generally unsuccessful submarines with which to context any Allied threat to the German coast. Typical of this type is the 'Molch' class of one-bmanboats, of which some 390 were placed in service. Unlike some other midget submarine classes, which were limited to flooded-down operation, the type was designed for completely submerged operation, and its armament comprised two 21in (533mm) torpedoes.

steamed into the Firth of Forth and surrendered its ships to the British. At much the same time, German U-boats were surrendering at a number of other ports as the British demanded the elimination of the German naval threat that had played so prominent a part in the build-up to World War I but had proved so limited during the war. The British were always conscious during the war that a major German success in a single battle, such as the Battle of Jutland in May/June 1916, could have altered the strategic balance of power, but the High Seas Fleet proved to be a potential rather than an actual threat, as Germany's surface fleet was bedevilled by internal dissension, a divided command structure, and mutiny. By the start of World War I the German navy had become the second largest navy in the world but, overshadowed throughout the war by the army, it totally failed to live up to its promise.

The exception to this general rule was the German submarine force, which grew from humble beginnings at the start of the war to become the single largest threat to the continued survival of Britain as a fighting power in 1917-18. Admiral von Tirpitz, the creator of the modern German navy, would have been appalled by the failure of the surface force, but might well have been proud of the performance of the submarine arm, which nearly achieved decisive results despite the indifferent and often dangerous characteristics of the U-boats of the period.

Exactly seven months after its surrender, the majority of the High Seas Fleet's surface ships were sunk by their crews, who were prohibited from

*Name ship of a class of three 'pocket battleships', the* Deutschland *was renamed as the* Lützow *in November 1939 . The ship survived until April 1945 before being sunk by British bombers.*

returning to Germany. At a stroke this denied the victorious Allies a large number of modern and well-designed German ships, and also denied some of the honour of the German navy, which felt that it had found a symbol of resistance that would be important in the days ahead as the service sought to re-establish itself.

The Treaty of Versailles that in 1919 formalised the end of Germany's part in World War I dictated that the Germany rising from the ashes of the war should have a navy limited to eight pre-dreadnought battleships and some smaller vessels, but no modern ships or submarines. The most important aspect of this limitation on the size and modernity of the new German navy was that it caused German warship designers and builders to lose touch with all real aspects of modern warship practice at a time when rapid developments were in the offing.

Unlike the army and clandestine air force, the navy could not circumvent the restrictions by training men or building ships in other countries, and therefore had to content itself in the short term with developing a theoretical model of how it had lost the naval war of World War I and therefore how it might fare more successfully in any future war.

Like the other branches of the German armed forces, overt or covert, the navy felt that Germany's position as one of the world's most important nations demanded larger and more capable forces, and even before the rise to power of the Nazi party in 1928, the first moves in the direction of an enlarged and more modern navy became apparent with the laying down in 1928 of the first of three *Panzerschiffe* (armoured ships) that later became known in the English-speaking world as 'pocket battleships'. The nature of the German navy's longer-term plans should have been clear from the nature of these ships: the navy of the Weimar Republic was essentially restricted in capability to army support operations in the Baltic Sea, but the new 'pocket battleships' were clearly commerce-raiding warships intended for long-range operations on the open seas. The ships were intermediate in size and capability between heavy cruisers and capital ships, and as such were designed to outfight any ships they could not outrun, and to outrun any ships they could not outfight. The ships were a reflection of the ideas of theorists such as Vizeadmiral Wolfgang Wegener, who suggested that the defeat of Britain could be achieved only if Germany broke out of the British stranglehold in the North Sea by taking Norway or Iceland for the creation of the bases that would allow German commerce raiders to wreak havoc on British maritime lines of communication.

Thus a small start had been made in the rebuilding of German naval strength before the rise to power of the Nazi party under Adolf Hitler. The naval commander-in-chief from 1928 was Admiral Erich Raeder, an officer who had made his mark on German naval affairs as the chief-of-staff to Admiral Franz von Hipper, commander of the High Seas Fleet's battle-cruiser force in World War I. Despite his professional background in one of the more ambitious elements of the High Seas Fleet, Raeder was in no way

*Hitler takes a salute from the light cruiser* Leipzig *during a fleet review at Kiel in 1933. The German light cruiser force was unable to achieve anything of note in World War II as it could not operate effectively in the North Sea in face of overwhelmingly superior British strength, and its ships lacked the range for operations in the North Atlantic with their larger brethren.*

**Freiwillig zur**

# KRIEGSMARINE

*A recruitment poster calls for volunteers for the German navy, emphasis being placed on the submarine arm that retained a very high level of morale throughout the war despite its appalling losses.*

a dashing officer in the mould of Admiral Sir David Beatty, who had commanded the British battle-cruiser force during much of World War I, but rather an officer whose main attributes were caution and systematic thought. Raeder's main concerns were therefore not the rapid creation of a navy capable of a maritime *Blitzkrieg* along the lines advocated by Wegener, but rather the establishment of a more traditionally shaped navy with the right organisational framework and the steady design and construction of the correct blend of warships optimised for the surface role but not ignoring the underwater role.

Raeder also appreciated that progress in the development of the navy was wholly dependent on the ever-shifting moods of Hitler, whose thinking on naval matters was conditioned largely by his attitude to Britain at any given time. In overall terms, Hitler planned to secure Germany's position as the major power of Europe, and only then proceed toward world domination. In the shorter term, therefore, it was in Germany's best interests to reach an accommodation with Britain, in which Germany would receive primacy

*The V-80 was an experimental submarine used for the development of the Walter propulsion system using the decomposition of concentrated hydrogen peroxide for considerably enhanced underwater speed and range.*

within Europe whilst allowing Britain to maintain its world position as the head of its huge empire. Such an accommodation could be achieved, in Hitler's estimation, by a guarantee that Germany would not seek to rival Britain in naval and colonial matters in the fashion that had pushed the two countries toward war in the period leading up to 1914.

At the beginning of his time as German leader, Hitler was optimistic that he could arrive at such an accommodation with Britain, but during the mid-1930s this optimism was gradually turned into pessimism by what he saw as British obstructionism towards Germany's 'legitimate aspirations'. Planning for a longer-term navy to rival that of the British navy had already been undertaken, but the combination of British 'obstructionism' and its apparent decadence (as revealed in its joining with France in the signature of the Munich agreement of September 1938 that cost Czechoslovakia its Sudetenland border regions with Germany) persuaded Hitler that the time was ripe for the acceleration of the German naval construction effort. This was the spur for the creation of the 'Plan Z' programme for the establishment of a navy that would be capable of Atlantic operations through its possession

*Seen here in 1938, the* Gneisenau *was an impressive battle-cruiser completed in that year and later used for commerce raider cruises before being badly damaged in February 1942 and decommissioned.*

of 13 battleships, four aircraft carriers, 33 cruisers and 250 U-boats, all of the very latest design. It was confidently believed that the completion of 'Plan Z' would allow Germany to challenge Britain, and possibly the USA, in the Atlantic during 1944.

Believing that France and Britain would not go to war with Germany over the matter, Hitler had few qualms about ordering the invasion of Poland in September 1939, thereby precipitating World War II and ultimately the end not only of himself but also of the Third Reich. In the short term, however, the successes of the German army and air forces seemed to indicate that Hitler had been right in essence if not in fact, for British and French intervention in the war was wholly ineffectual. This helped to disguise the fact that the German navy was not ready for war, for its whole development plan had been based on a start of hostilities no sooner than 1942 and probably only in 1944.

The German navy thus found itself with a small and unbalanced surface force that laboured under the same geographical disadvantages as the German navy of World War I: both of the German navy's access routes to the Atlantic, via the English Channel and the North Sea, were dominated by the Royal Navy, and all its merchant marine was rendered virtually useless by the same fact. Moreover, merchant ships currently outside Germany could not in most cases return home and thus fell to the British, who gratefully accepted these accessions to their own merchant marine.

It was only by turning a British flank or alternatively by creating a navy that could challenge the British superiority, that the German navy could now undertake anything of real utility. The latter option was impossible within the foreseeable future as Germany lacked the production facilities to turn out suitable ships, complete with armament and armour, at a time when most production was being concentrated on the army and air force that were

*Below: The* Scharnhorst *was sister ship of the* Gneisenau, *and was lost in action against superior British forces in December 1943 in conditions that prevented the effective fighting of the ship.*

*Opposite: The* Gneisenau *had a powerful main armament of nine 11in (280mm) guns in three triple turrets (a superfiring pair forward and a single turret aft), but was somewhat limited by the Germans' failure to develop effective dual-purpose guns and fire-control systems: this necessitated the installation of a secondary battery of twelve 5.9in (150mm) anti-ship guns and a tertiary battery of fourteen 4.13in (105mm) anti-aircraft guns each with its own fire-control system.*

currently achieving military wonders. The German navy was therefore compelled to think of ways in which it might turn a British flank, either in reality or metaphorically.

At the outbreak of World War II, the German navy comprised two excellent battle-cruisers (*Scharnhorst* and *Gneisenau*) that could not hope to survive against British battleships, three 'pocket battleships' (*Deutschland*, *Lützow* and *Graf Spee*) that were optimised for raiding rather than fleet actions, two heavy cruisers (*Admiral Hipper* and *Blücher*) that were fine ships of their type but inadequate for involvement in fleet actions, six light cruisers, 34 destroyers and torpedo boats, and 57 submarines.

On the other side of the North Sea, the British could deploy 15 battleships and battle-cruisers, six aircraft carriers, 59 heavy and light cruisers, hundreds of destroyers and other light warships, and 38 submarines. The French could contribute seven battleships and battle-cruisers, two aircraft carriers, 19 heavy and light cruisers, a large number of lighter warships such as destroyers, and submarines. The British and French included in their totals a numbers of older and less capable vessels, and because of their colonial responsibilities were compelled to keep substantial forces in areas far from Europe, but even so their naval strength in home waters was vastly superior to that of the Germans.

The outbreak of war in September 1939 was rightly appreciated by Raeder as having made 'Plan Z' totally obsolete, and he therefore ordered the cancellation of all major warship construction, including the aircraft carrier *Graf Zeppelin*, except for the completion of two battleships (*Bismarck* and *Tirpitz*) and one heavy cruiser (*Prinz Eugen*).

The limited strength available to him compelled Raeder in the early months of the war to restrict the activities of his surface force to commerce raiding. The *Deutschland*, *Scharnhorst* and *Gneisenau* sortied into the North Atlantic but achieved little success. So it was only the *Graf Spee* that made any real impact with a successful cruise in the Indian and South Atlantic

Oceans until she was scuttled in December 1939, after an inconclusive skirmish with one New Zealand and two British cruisers in the Battle of the River Plate, to avoid being overwhelmed by what her captain thought was an overwhelmingly superior Allied force.

This temporarily ended the German surface raider effort, whose effect on the Allies could have been considerable had it continued, not so much through the destruction of the merchant shipping that would have inevitably succumbed to the raiders but through the dilution of Allied naval strength. In October 1939, for example, the Royal Navy's main surface forces had lost the use of nine battleships and battle-cruisers, five aircraft carriers and a number of smaller warships, as the Admiralty sought to find and destroy just two 'pocket battleships' currently at sea on commerce-raiding cruises. Germany had so few major surface warships, however, and Raeder felt that the threat to these vessels was too great for their loss to be risked.

The whole balance of the naval war altered in June 1940, for the defeat of France in that month combined with the seizure of Norway to provide the German navy with a reduced opposition as the French navy was out of the battle, and with ports and secure anchorages in western France and northern Norway that outflanked the British domination of the North Sea and English Channel. A further diminution of the threat faced by the German navy's major surface vessels came in the same month, when Italy declared war on the Allies and at a stroke caused the diversion of many British ships for service in the Mediterranean.

Despite this setback, the Royal Navy still had a comfortable margin of superiority over the German navy in home waters, as exemplified in the Norwegian campaign (April/June 1940) when the latter had suffered heavy losses including the heavy cruiser *Blücher*, the light cruisers *Karlsruhe* and *Königsberg*, and 10 destroyers, as well as substantial damage to the *Scharnhorst*, *Gneisenau*, *Lützow* (formerly *Deutschland*) and *Admiral Hipper*.

In the summer of 1940, therefore, the navy had virtually no surface strength so it was perhaps fortunate for the Germans that the Luftwaffe failed to win the Battle of Britain, and therefore ended all possibility, at least in the short term, of a German invasion of Britain that could not have been supported in any meaningful manner by the German navy. Ironically, however, Germany now had the best naval position in overall strategic terms, but had virtually no ships with which to exploit this position. All that the German navy could essay was a continuance of the commerce-raiding effort by single ships or a very small group of ships. This caused considerable worry to Britain, which was highly concerned about the vulnerability of her maritime lines of communication, but was never any real threat to overall British naval superiority. It is arguable that the German navy's single major success in this period was that fear of the depredations that might be caused

*The battleship* Bismarck *was in many ways a superb vessel, but her apparent strength was belied by a number of poor design features resulting largely from the German navy's lack of experience in battleship design and operation in the period following World War I.*

*The* Prinz Eugen *was a superb heavy cruiser, and is here exemplified by one of her quadruple 20mm anti-aircraft gun mountings in action against British bombers attacking her base at Brest, the north-west French port that was a constant target when occupied by German heavy warships.*

by its limited surface forces meant the retention in British waters of sizeable parts of the Royal Navy's surface strength.

Even so, it would not have been wise to disperse all these ships to other tasks, as was revealed by the cruise of the new battleship *Bismarck* and her heavy cruiser escort, *Prinz Eugen*, in May 1941.

In concert with the commerce raids by a limited number of heavy warships, which were the only surface vessels with the range to undertake the task, the German navy also sent out numbers of secret raiders, which were middle-sized merchant ships converted with concealed medium-calibre guns and torpedoes as well as provision for the carriage and laying of large numbers of mines. These ships, which were also carefully outfitted with repair facilities, additional stores, and large quantities of food and other consumables, were intended to avoid any confrontation with Allied warships and concentrate their attentions on Allied merchant shipping, which was to be sunk or captured so that a prize crew could attempt the journey back to

*The* Prinz Eugen *was the only major German surface warship to survive World War II, and was then expended in American nuclear weapon tests.*

Germany. These long-range vessels were supported by supply ships carrying ammunition, fuel and other necessities for transfer at secret mid-ocean rendezvous points.

These raiders, of which there were only seven, operated mainly in the Atlantic, Indian and Pacific Oceans to the south, east and north-west of Australia, and succeeded in sinking 133 merchant ships with a gross tonnage of 829,650 tons (which was more than twice the tonnage achieved by the warship raiders), and also one light cruiser and one armed merchant cruiser, as well as damaging two other armed merchant cruisers. Preying on ships not travelling on convoy, the success of the secret raiders offered no real long-term threat to the Allies, but tied up large numbers of warships that could more profitably have been employed elsewhere.

The most successful raid by a single German major warship was undertaken by the 'pocket battleship' *Admiral Scheer* between October 1940, when she sailed from Brunsbüttel, and April 1941 when she returned to Kiel after a cruise through the North and South Atlantic and the Indian Ocean, in the course of which she sank 16 ships totalling 99,060 tons.

The last successful raid undertaken by the German major warships occurred in January 1941, when the battle-cruisers *Scharnhorst* and *Gneisenau* sortied into the North Atlantic via the Denmark Strait at the beginning of an operation that lasted until March. The two ships achieved a number of successes (22 ships totalling 115,625 tons), but were prevented from scoring more 'kills' by the escort of convoys at this time by British capital ships, against whose larger-calibre guns the German captains sensibly decided not to enter into combat. Even so, the German raid caused great disruption to British naval plans.

In overall terms, the German surface raiders cannot be accounted a major success, although at least the cruises of the secret raiders were cost-effective. If the Germans had bided their time and had been less unfortunate with damage to their ships, however, they could have assembled a major strike force for an Atlantic operation with the battleship *Bismarck*, which was a more capable capital ship than any single British counterpart, supported by the battle-cruisers *Scharnhorst* and *Gneisenau*, the heavy cruisers *Admiral Hipper* and *Prinz Eugen*, and possibly the 'pocket battleship' *Admiral Scheer*. The foray of a force of this strength would have severely strained the British, who would have found their command of the Atlantic severely threatened unless they withdrew major units from the Mediterranean, thereby offering the Italian navy an opportunity to score a major success. In the event, the advent of the *Bismarck* and *Prinz Eugen* in German waters coincided with repairs to the *Scharnhorst* and *Gneisenau* in Brest, and refits of the *Admiral Scheer* and *Admiral Hipper* in Germany.

It was under these conditions that the *Bismarck* and *Prinz Eugen* sortied alone into the North Atlantic during May 1941. Departing from the Baltic Sea, the two ships evaded British patrols as they headed up the coast of occupied Norway and round the north of Iceland to emerge into the North Atlantic via the Denmark Strait between Iceland and Greenland. The German force, under the command of Vizeadmiral Günther Lütjens, encountered the British capital ships *Hood* and *Prince of Wales*. The elderly battle-cruiser *Hood*, pride of the Royal Navy, succumbed to accurate long-range fire that also damaged the *Prince of Wales* before the German ships, shadowed by British cruisers, moved away into the North Atlantic.

The threat of the German raiding force was taken extremely seriously by the British, who responded by detaching three capital ships and one aircraft carrier, as well as a squadron of cruisers, from the Home Fleet in British waters, and then one capital ship, one aircraft carrier and one cruiser from Force H at Gibraltar. Even so, it was providential that a British flying boat sighted the German battleship, now on her own after breaking contact with the shadowing British cruisers and detaching the *Prinz Eugen* to return to France separately, and that a torpedo bomber attack then damaged the battleship's rudder, allowing the British heavy ships to make contact and then sink the *Bismarck* with all but 110 of her 2,300-man crew.

Yet without this monumental British

*Denied the chance to operate effectively in the North Sea as a result of British naval strength, the limited numbers of small and large destroyers available to the Germans could only be operated to any significant effect in areas that were also free of British air strength, most notably northern Norway and the Bay of Biscay.*

*Seen here behind its torpedo net defences in a Norwegian fjord, the* Lützow *was the 'pocket battleship'* Deutschland, *which had been renamed in November 1939 in response to fears that the destruction of a ship named after the Fatherland would be a blow to morale. In 1940 the ship was reclassified as a heavy cruiser.*

effort, the *Bismarck* and *Prinz Eugen* would have been free to wreak total havoc on the British convoys plying the Atlantic. Thus Operation 'Weserübung', as the *Bismarck*'s ill-fated sortie had been codenamed, resulted in Germany's greatest naval victory of World War II and also its greatest disaster, in the form of the sinking of the *Hood* and the loss of the *Bismarck* respectively. Moreover, the loss of the *Bismarck* caused a major shift in German naval policy when Hitler, so incensed by the loss of the German battleship that he announced that 'On land I am a hero, but at sea I am a coward', overruled Raeder and forbade any further warship forays into the Atlantic.

Hitler, never a believer in the desirability of a major surface navy, decided at this time that the emphasis of the German navy's construction, manning and operations would be shifted heavily from the surface fleet to the submarine arm. Raeder was quietly furious, not only because it marked the end of the branch of the service in which he had particular interest but also because it revealed the further decline of his position *vis-à-vis* the Führer. With hindsight, it is possible to appreciate that Hitler was absolutely right in his decision, however, for the surface ships consumed vast quantities of valuable fuel, required skilled manpower that could be better used elsewhere, and were producing a steadily declining return for the great investment they required. This last factor occurred for a number of reasons: the German navy lacked the number of large warships required for an effective surface force; the battleship and battle-cruiser had already started their decline into obsolescence as effective capital ships; and the British were now considerably better-equipped to deal with the surface warship raider through their operation of large numbers of radar-equipped long-range aircraft, that could detect the raiders and call in British capital ships or aircraft carriers while relays of aircraft shadowed the German target. Moreover, even when they were in harbour, the surviving German ships were constantly harassed and attacked by British bombers, which were increasing in numbers and were now of the four-engined types that were able to deliver far heavier and more effective bomb loads.

By Hitler's express order, therefore, from the spring of 1942 the remaining large German warships were restricted to operations in the Baltic, where they faced a currently indifferent threat from Soviet warplanes and submarines, and off Norway, which Hitler constantly believed was a target for a major British amphibious invasion. The location of German ships in Norway would thus help in the defence of this region (which was considered essential to Germany's long-term interests as it was the channel by which the country received most of its supplies of Swedish iron ore and other minerals), and also provide a striking force for the interception, beyond the effective range of Allied air patrols, of convoys carrying Allied supplies to northern Russia.

As part of this decision to concentrate German naval surface strength in the Baltic and Norway, it was decided that the *Scharnhorst*, *Gneisenau* and *Prinz Eugen* would make a dash up the English Channel from Brest to bases in Germany. Undertaken over three days in February 1942, this Operation 'Cerberus' was a triumph in its own right as the ships steamed at high speed, under cover of a massive umbrella of Luftwaffe fighters, right through the

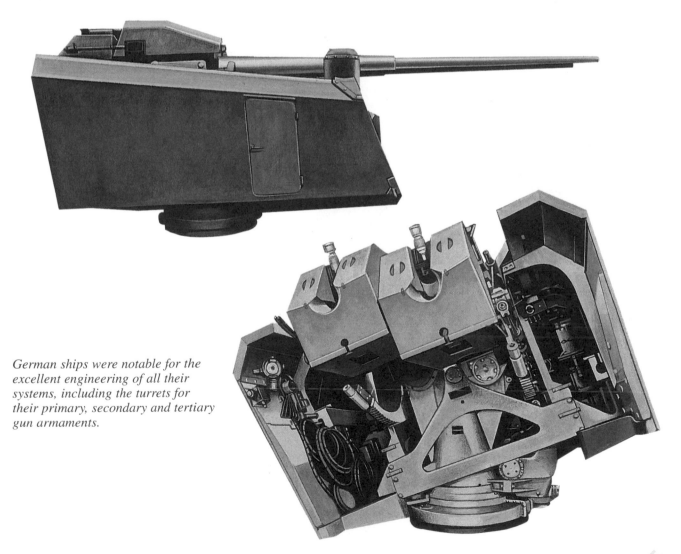

*German ships were notable for the excellent engineering of all their systems, including the turrets for their primary, secondary and tertiary gun armaments.*

*The* Graf Spee *was the first of the German navy's three 'pocket battleships' to be lost when her captain scuttled the ship in December 1939 in the erroneous belief that his exit from the estuary of the River Plate was barred by an overwhelmingly superior British force.*

British 'back yard' without Royal Navy interception until the ships were off the French/Belgian frontier. Further attacks were made by British warships and aircraft in the most courageous and costly fashion, but none of these attacks achieved significant result, and the German ships reached port safely even though the *Scharnhorst* and *Gneisenau* had been damaged off the Dutch coast by mines. The German propaganda machine made great play with this 'Channel dash', which certainly caught the British unawares, but the episode nonetheless marked the end of an era for the German navy.

The first sortie under the new operational scheme was a total failure that further sapped the morale of the German surface force. This operation took place late in December 1942, when the *Admiral Lützow* and *Admiral Hipper* sortied with six destroyers to tackle a British convoy but were driven off by a somewhat weaker British escort force. The failure confirmed Hitler's belief that he had made the right decision in curtailing the operational scope of his navy's surface force and, coinciding with the 6th Army's failure in its attempt to survive in Stalingrad, incensed the Führer to such a degree that in January 1943 he ordered the scrapping of all Germany's major surface ships so that their weapons could be used to bolster the anti-invasion defences of Norway and their manpower reallocated to more worthwhile tasks.

Grossadmiral Raeder's stock with the Führer had begun to decline in the summer of 1940, when the naval commander-in-chief objected to the concentration of so much industrial capacity on preparations for the following year's invasion of the USSR, which did not involve the navy in any significant manner. The naval failures of the following 2½ years had further reduced Hitler's confidence in his naval chief, so when Raeder offered his resignation in the aftermath of Hitler's scrapping order, Hitler readily accepted it and appointed as his successor Admiral Karl Dönitz, commander of the German navy's submarine arm.

As the head of a branch of the service that had scored major successes and was currently threatening Britain's survival, Dönitz was able to secure a far more workable relationship with the German leader, and was even able to persuade Hitler to rescind his scrapping order: one of the keys to Dönitz's success with Hitler was his appreciation that he should not be as distant,

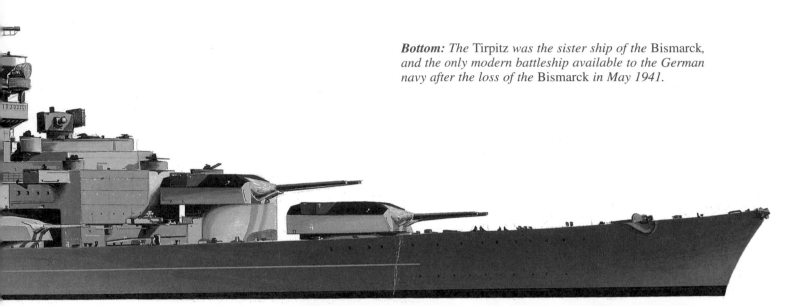

*Bottom: The* Tirpitz *was the sister ship of the* Bismarck, *and the only modern battleship available to the German navy after the loss of the* Bismarck *in May 1941.*

either emotionally or physically, as Raeder had been, and thereby should be able to work directly with the German leader as a means of warding off the efforts of men such as Reichsmarschall Hermann Goering, commander-in-chief of the Luftwaffe, to belittle the navy in the hope of diverting its assets to the use of their own services. So successful was Dönitz in striking up a good relationship with Hitler that, in the Führer's will, Dönitz was appointed as successor.

The success of Dönitz in persuading Hitler to rescind the scrapping order did not mean, however, that a major sea-going role was also restored to the major ships of the surface force, but merely that they would be maintained as a means of strengthening the defences of Norway against Allied amphibious invasion. Despite this fact, the Allies still saw the ships as a major threat – not to any invasion of Norway, which was never seriously planned but was maintained as a means of persuading the Germans to keep large land, sea and air forces in the country – but to the Arctic

*These two German fleet destroyers were half-sisters within the 'Type 36A' class. The Z24 (below) was of the original eight-strong design with a full-load displacement of 3,600 tons and a primary armament of five 5.9in (150mm) guns in one twin and three single mountings, while the Z37 of the later seven-strong 'Narvik' class subvariant introduced a number of improvements suggested by continued wartime experience.*

convoys that were in fact very much a secondary threat in Hitler's thinking. This, then, was the reason for the spate of British bomber, carrierborne warplane and midget submarine attacks on the largest ship in Norwegian waters, *Bismarck*'s sistership *Tirpitz*, and also for the extraordinary combined naval and Commando attack on the drydock at St Nazaire in western France, which was the only facility of its type in western Europe large enough to accommodate the *Tirpitz*.

The German navy's last major surface battle took place late in December 1943 off the North Cape, which marks the extreme northern tip of Norway. In this Battle of the Barents Sea the *Scharnhorst*, which had sortied with the *Admiral Lützow* and six destroyers to intercept an Allied convoy to north Russia, was herself intercepted in company with three destroyers after Vizeadmiral Oskar Kummetz had divided his force in an effort to capture the Allied convoy in the jaws of a pincer movement. Unknown to the Germans, the British were covering the convoy with one battleship, three cruisers and five destroyers. Now caught between the battleship *Duke of York* and one light cruiser to the south-west and two heavy cruisers to the north-east, the *Scharnhorst* went down after a battering from the British guns, only 36 of her 1,900-man crew being saved.

This left the *Tirpitz* as the only capital ship still available to the Germans, and she was lost in November 1944 when she capsized in a Norwegian fjord after being hit by British 12,000lb (5,443kg) 'Tallboy' bombs. All of Germany's other surviving large warships were now used either as training

*The* Prinz Eugen *arrived in British waters en route to the USA after the end of World War II.*

ships or as monitors for the support of German army operations on the southern shore of the Baltic Sea. The *Gneisenau* had been paid off after bomb damage in 1942, and in 1945 the same fate befell the *Admiral Lützow*, *Admiral Scheer* and *Admiral Hipper*. The only large German warship to survive World War II was the magnificent *Prinz Eugen*, which was then expended as a target in American nuclear weapon tests after the war.

Dönitz was the major protagonist of the German submarine arm, and was exactly the right man to succeed Raeder as this arm had entirely replaced the surface vessel force as the German navy's primary asset by the middle of 1942. In many respects this mirrored the situation that had developed in World War I, when the German navy had begun the conflict with the submarine arm as the junior partner of the surface force, but then had been compelled to reverse this priority as the surface force was driven to effective impotence after mid-1916 and the submarine arm went from strength to strength as the sole German harrier of Britain's maritime lines of communication and surface warships.

The young Dönitz served in submarines, or U-boats, for two years during World War I, and maintained his interest in such craft as he remained with the navy of the Weimar Republic which was prohibited from any involvement with submarines. When the Nazi party acceded to power in January 1933, clandestine work on the design of submarines was accelerated and revealed, for in the development of a submarine arm the Nazi party saw a comparatively quick and comparatively cheap method of developing a

*The* Bismarck *rides through the North Atlantic swell in May 1941, somewhat low in the bows after suffering damage and taking on water, in the aftermath of the Battle of the Denmark Strait in which its accurate long-range gunfire sank the* Hood*, still the pride of the Royal Navy.*

a strike force that could achieve decisive results along the lines of the campaign fought in World War I.

The first German submarines were small and relatively ineffective boats that were little better than the U-boats with which Germany had finished World War I. Gradually the quality and number of boats was improved, but by the outbreak of World War II only 22 of the currently available 34 submarines were of the ocean-going rather than coastal types. Despite this numerical poverty, great things were expected of the submarine arm as it possessed four major advantages, namely the dedicated leadership of Dönitz, the aggressive tradition inherited from the submarine arm of World War I, the support of Hitler and the Nazi party, and the productive capability of German shipyards, which were admirably suited to the task of producing submarines by a method that was soon of the production-line type. Submarine production increased rapidly after the start of the war, not only because operational conditions dictated an accelerated production rate but also because Raeder's cancellation of 'Plan Z' allowed plans to be formulated for the monthly construction of 30 rather than 20 boats, the majority of them of the 'Type VIIC' class of 770-ton ocean-going submarines.

Production of the required boats was only half of the equation, however, for Dönitz not only had to find the men to man the new submarines but also had to create training, maintenance and operational infrastructures capable of handling the expansion of the underwater arm. Dönitz was also careful not to commit his larger number of boats too soon, for experience in the first months of the war confirmed that the British had continued to learn much about anti-submarine warfare after World War I, and were a considerably more potent force than they had been in 1918.

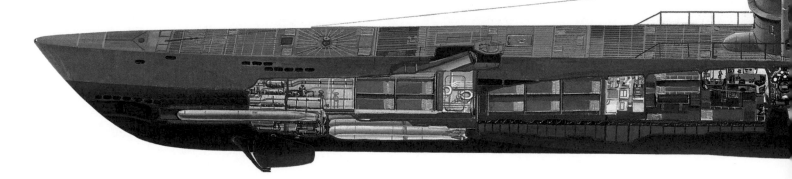

A convoy system was established from the beginning of hostilities, and even though the British held too high an opinion of their ASDIC (now generally known as sonar) equipment for the detection of submerged submarines, their more modern escorts were still highly capable anti-submarine types. The main problems affecting the British were not so much technical, therefore, even though there were many technical matters that had to be addressed, but rather the very scale of the problem, with many thousands of merchant ships being marshalled into convoys and then escorted to and from British ports. The problem was eased initially by the limited range of the German submarines, so the middle portions of any oceanic transit required only modest anti-submarine rather than anti-surface ship escort, allowing greater concentration of the escorts in the bottleneck regions, such as the North-West and South-West Approaches, that could easily be reached by the German submarines. As the number of submarines increased and technical development continued, however, the size and scope of the threat placed an enormous burden on the escort forces as submarines could be built more quickly and cheaply than the escorts designed to fight them. For this reason therefore, the British decided that their pre-war destroyer classes, which were designed primarily for the anti-ship role, should be replaced in the escort role by larger numbers of smaller, cheaper and more readily built dedicated escorts of the destroyer escort, frigate, sloop and corvette types.

These German and British developments conditioned the nature of the submarine war in the Atlantic Ocean. On the one hand, the Germans sought to build and man submarines of types increasingly well suited to operating and tactical conditions prevalent in the Atlantic Ocean so that they could intercept and destroy strategically vital numbers of the merchant ships on which the British were dependent initially for survival (and later the Allies were dependent for the build-up and maintenance of the forces to be used in any invasion of Europe). On the other hand, the British and the Americans strove to build and man both replacement merchant ships and an increasing number of dedicated anti-submarine escorts to protect these merchant ships through a combination of superior tactics, upgraded sensors (sonar, radar and direction-finders) and more capable weapons. Such weaponry included projectors that fired patterns of bombs ahead of the ship while the target submarine was still held in the sonar beam and thus complemented the traditional depth charge that was dropped over the stern or fired over the beam against target submarines that had been lost to sonar.

The task of the escorts was made more difficult by the fact that they had to face the German surface raiders and often had to counter German bombers. The latter threat was alleviated to a significant degree only in 1942

*This cutaway illustration of a typical German U-boat reveals the extremely tight packing of machinery and equipment into the small pressure hull, and therefore the limited space that was left for the crew, for whom habitability became an obsession on long operational cruises.*

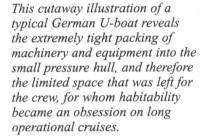

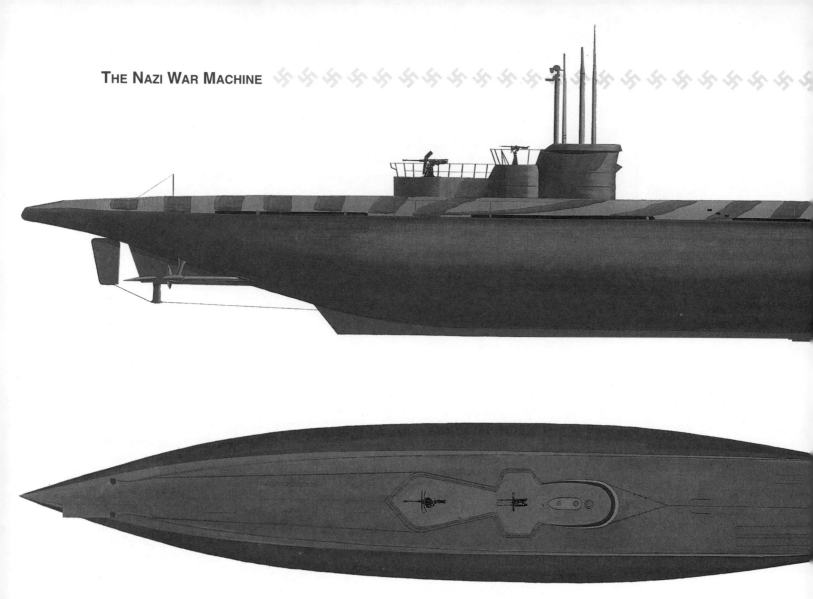

with the advent of the escort or 'jeep' carrier, which was a small aircraft carrier based on a merchant ship hull and propulsion arrangement, and designed to carry a small number of fighters that could drive off or destroy the German bombers and long-range reconnaissance aircraft (which were used to detect convoys and vector 'wolf packs' of submarines towards them), and a larger number of anti-submarine aircraft that could tackle the submarines at some distance from the threatened convoy.

The Battle of the Atlantic therefore encompassed a conflict between two technologies. While the Germans sought to produce submarines with improved range and speed, better protection, and larger numbers of more effective weapons, and which when submerged were quieter and capable of diving to greater depths, the Allies concentrated on the creation of longer-ranged and more effective methods of detecting and localising the German submarines (preferably whilst running on the surface), so that they could be engaged at greater distances from convoys and with weapons made more effective in terms of stand-off range and lethality.

Such developments were, of course, still in the future as the submarine war began in 1939. Initially, this aspect of World War II was fought at a low level of intensity as each side sought to find the best methods of putting pre-war developments into wartime practice.

The German submarine arm began the war with comparatively few operational boats. The smaller of these U-boats were used mainly for the laying of minefields off British ports, in the process causing the losses of many ships and requiring the detachment of British warships from other

*Germany's U-boats with conventional diesel/electric propulsion were always notable for their good surfaced speed and range, but also for the limited underwater speed and range possible with their electric motors and modest battery capacity. The fact that such boats had to run on the surface as they recharged their batteries meant that they became increasingly liable to attack by Allied anti-submarine aircraft, and this resulted in a proliferation of their anti-aircraft gun armament to the further detriment of streamlining and therefore underwater speed.*

tasks for the support of coastal convoys and the clearance of mined areas. The larger U-boats roamed farther afield, and soon began to accrue useful tallies of tonnages sunk. These sinkings were mainly of merchant vessels, but on occasion included major British warships such as the aircraft carrier *Courageous* that was torpedoed by the *U-29* in September 1939, and then the battleship *Royal Oak* that was torpedoed in the following month by the *U-47* under the command of one of Germany's first and greatest U-boat 'aces', Kapitänleutnant Günther Prien. The loss of the aircraft carrier was a major blow at the tactical level, but while the sinking of the battleship was less important in overall terms as she was obsolescent and used only for local defence, the fact that she was attacked and sunk on the supposedly impenetrable anchorage at Scapa Flow in the Orkney Islands came as a greater emotional shock to the British and was therefore a considerable propaganda victory for the Germans.

The first weeks of the submarine war were fought in general by the dictates of international law but, as had been the case in World War I, it soon became apparent that such rules were genuinely impossible to implement effectively. This fact was confirmed by the September 1939 sinking of the liner *Athenia* without prior warning, resulting in the deaths of 112 out of 1,400 passengers as the ship was sailing from Liverpool to Montreal. Raeder was one of the first German officers to appreciate that the old rules were now obsolete in practical terms, and managed to persuade the more cautious Hitler, who still hoped that an accommodation with Britain might be possible, to permit a policy of submarine warfare unrestricted by rules: Raeder was greatly assisted in his successful effort to convince Hitler by the fact that the British were now arming their merchant ships, and by the fact of the USA's neutrality declaration (which interdicted a large part of the western Atlantic to the submarines) and also of its November lifting of the arms embargo in a fashion that aided the Allies. By 1940, therefore, the submarine war was one in which no holds were barred.

By the end of 1939, the four months of World War II had cost the Allies 114 merchant ships totalling 420,000 tons, and this was clearly no real threat to their merchant marines, of which the British and French were by far the largest and best able to cope with losses at this rate: the British merchant marine, for example, totalled more than 21 million tons. British and French confidence was heightened during the early months of 1940, moreover, as Hitler switched production priority from submarines to land weapons for the forthcoming German invasions of Denmark, Norway, the Netherlands, Belgium and France, and then the number of boats available to the German submarine arm declined as a result of the Norwegian campaign, in which they were used to shield German amphibious invasion forces and then to intercept and destroy any Allied amphibious or naval response. The Norwegian campaign was a setback for the submarine arm for two reasons, however, for it suffered losses and also underwent a period of intense dissatisfaction as its latest torpedoes failed to detonate as a result of problems with the new type of magnetic rather than impact pistols.

This feeling of dissatisfaction soon evaporated as the implications of the land campaigns of April to June 1940 became clear: the German navy now had access to bases from the northern tip of Norway to the border of France with Spain, and the advent of Italy into the war as a German ally also opened the possibility of Mediterranean operations from Italian bases. The most important of these new bases were those in western France, which offered easy access to the Atlantic Ocean without the long, dangerous and often uncomfortable trip through the North Sea and round the northernmost point of the British Isles. The additional radius thus provided to the boats meant

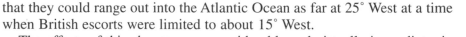

that they could range out into the Atlantic Ocean as far at 25° West at a time when British escorts were limited to about 15° West.

The effects of this change were considerable and virtually immediate: in June 1940, the submarines sank 58 Allied ships totalling 284,000 tons, but by September the figure had risen to 63 ships totalling 350,000 tons. The rise in sinkings was itself important, but just as significant to the British was the fact that they now had a smaller pool of merchant ships as the French merchant marine was no longer available since the fall of France. There was still a great British fear of a German amphibious invasion, but the threat to the Atlantic shipping routes was considered somewhat more dangerous, and comparatively large numbers of escorts were switched from anti-invasion to convoy escort tasks. The British position was further strengthened in September 1940 by the decidedly anti-German decision of the American government to sign an agreement with Britain for the exchange of 50 old American destroyers, ill-suited to the modern anti-ship role but readily adaptable for the anti-submarine role, for leases to British air and naval bases in the western hemisphere, which the USA viewed as its own bailiwick.

Dönitz was happy that the rate of his boats' successes was rising, but he was still concerned that his force was in no position to inflict a decisive blow on the British as a result of the comparatively small number of submarines available (reaching a low point of only 21 ocean-going submarines in February 1941), the diversion of a number of boats to the Mediterranean in an effort to destroy the Royal Navy and British merchant marine in this Italian 'lake', and the poor weather in the North Atlantic. The German situation was worsened by the fact that British shipyards were beginning to achieve a notable increase in deliveries, with a swelling number of dedicated anti-submarine corvettes being completed; Canada was starting to provide a larger number of effective anti-submarine patrols by aircraft operating from its eastern seaboard; and the USA was veering still more strongly toward Britain in its interpretation of international and national law, including the passing of the Lend-Lease Act in March 1941, the taking of Greenland under US protection in April 1941, the garrisoning of Iceland by American forces from July 1941, and provision of anti-submarine escorts in its own 'security zone' to the west of Iceland from September 1941.

The astute Dönitz was aware of the implications of all these factors, but appreciated that the only one over which he had direct influence was the number of German submarines available. His own estimate was that he would need some 300 boats to encompass the defeat of the British by severing their maritime lines of communication, but at times he had available a mere one-tenth of this requirement. This was a severe impediment to the successful implementation of the 'wolf pack' tactic that Dönitz had decided was the best operational method for his submarines: this tactic was posited on the deployment on the major British sea lanes of packs of between 15 and 20 submarines, each pack being spaced to maximise the chances of a convoy being detected by one boat that would radio the information and shadow the convoy as the other members of the pack closed in to an interception position from which several concerted attacks could be launched, each involving a torrent of torpedoes rained on the British ships by submarines operating wherever possible on the surface, where their low silhouettes made visual, sonar and even radar detection difficult, and where the submarines' speed and agility were at least equal to those of the dedicated convoy escorts.

In the 12 months between December 1940 and November 1941, the German submarines sank 1,726,000 tons of Allied merchant shipping in the North Atlantic, but Dönitz was well aware that about two-thirds of this tonnage was represented by the sinking of ships sailing independently in a fashion that the British had virtually eliminated by the end of the period, that the Luftwaffe had managed to sink a greater tonnage with air attacks, and that the German navy's surface warship raids had also made a contribution. So while the situation was far from ideal from the submarine point of view, it was generally good for Germany as the rate of sinkings meant that the tonnage lost to the British now comfortably exceeded the rate at which British yards could replace it: by June 1941 the British had lost some 5.7 million tons and built only 800,000 tons.

The balance in the Battle of the Atlantic was swinging Germany's way, but Dönitz appreciated the probable temporary nature of this tendency in the light of Britain's accelerating escort production effort, the British introduction of longer range warplanes that could roam farther into the central Atlantic in their search for German submarines, the increasing sophistication of the British bomber attacks on the German reinforced-concrete submarine bases, the growing involvement of the technically neutral Americans and the Canadians on the western side of the Atlantic, and the inevitability of an Allied counter to the German bomber and aerial reconnaissance efforts.

The year 1941 therefore marked a period of transition between the somewhat tentative efforts typical of the war's early years and the emergence of the Battle of the Atlantic during 1942. By 1942 both sides had come to appreciate the overriding importance of this Battle to the final outcome of World War II, especially after the entry of the USA into the war on the Allied side in December 1941 and the checking of Germany's expansion in the western USSR during 1942. With stalemate on the Eastern Front, where the Soviets would clearly become stronger as the war continued, the full

*Costing comparatively little to build and easy to man, the midget submarine appealed strongly to the German navy in the later stages of World War II as a means of providing an effective defence of the German coast, but such boats were relatively ineffective and a reflection more of Germany's desperation than of any real operational analysis. This is an example of the 15-ton 'Type XXVIIB' or 'Seehund' class, which had a two-man crew, a conventional diesel/electric propulsion arrangement, and an armament of two 21in (533mm) torpedoes carried below the main hull.*

involvement of the Americans meant a greater flow of essential supplies to the United Kingdom and also the inevitability of an American build-up in Britain for an Allied invasion of France as a means of opening another strategic front against Germany.

In the short term, however, the entry of the USA into the war provided a second period of success for the U-boats. There was no black-out along the American east coast, which provided the low-lying submarines with targets silhouetted against the shore line, and the US Navy lacked the ships and experience to inaugurate an effective system of coastal convoys: the result was that the German submarines, supported in these long-range operations by 'milch cow' submarines that could transfer fuel and reload torpedoes at sea, had a virtually unhindered run of success as they sank nearly 500,000 tons of American shipping, much of it comprising vital oil tankers, between January and the end of March 1942. It was only in the early months of the summer that the US Navy was able to organise a convoy system along the American east coast, and in conjunction with improved co-operation from the US Army Air Forces and the US Coast Guard, of which the latter was now under US Navy operational control, this meant a rapid decline in the success of the

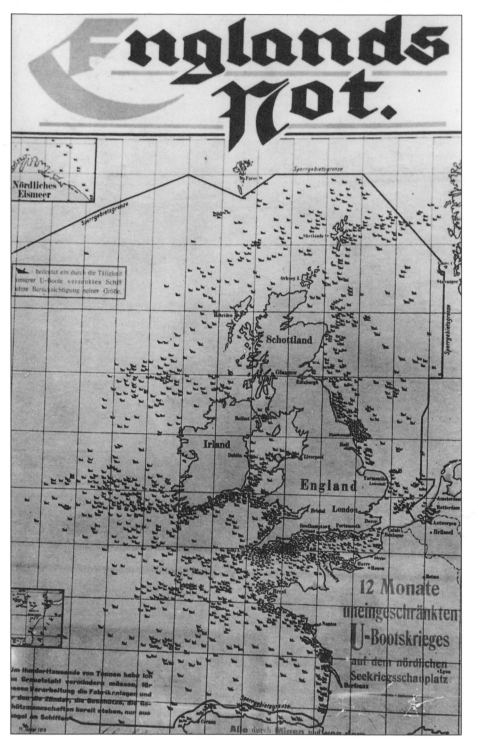

submarines, which were soon directed to switch their area of operations farther to the south, where the Caribbean Sea offered rich pickings (including large numbers of oil tankers and bauxite carriers) as well as the opportunity to intercept ships entering or emerging from the Panama Canal.

This expansion of the submarine war was made possible only by the belated expansion of the submarine building programme under the direct supervision of Albert Speer, Germany's new and highly capable minister of war production. By the summer of 1942, Dönitz was able to deploy some 150 submarines in many parts of the world. Considerable success was being achieved in the South Atlantic Ocean and the Caribbean Sea, but the most important operational area was still the North Atlantic, where the increase in

*This German propaganda 'chart' shows the positions in which German submarines had sunk British ships up to September 1940, in the period before the main part of the U-boat campaign moved farther west into the Atlantic Ocean.*

the number of available ocean-going submarines finally allowed Dönitz to introduce the larger size of 'wolf pack' he had long wanted. Offering greater capabilities in attack, but also more detectable as they grouped for the onslaught, these packs were generally allocated to the 'black hole' in the middle of the North Atlantic Ocean, which was a gap of some 600 miles (965km) in the air coverage possible by land-based aircraft operating from Canada, Iceland and Britain. The significance of the Germans' increased strength was reflected in the fact that, during the second half of 1942, the Allies lost to submarine attack 1,160 ships totalling 6,266,000 tons, and to other causes 504 ships totalling 1,524,000 tons. Even with the enormous capacity of the USA now turning out large numbers of merchant ships, there was currently no way that the Allies could replace ships at the rate that the Germans were sinking them, and the result was a major decline in the tonnage of food, oil and raw materials reaching the United Kingdom, where stocks of these essentials was plummeting to crisis levels. During 1942, the Germans lost only 85 boats.

Just as worrying as the losses up to this stage was the way in which these losses were occurring. Up to the beginning of 1942, most of the losses had been of ships sailing independently or otherwise separated from their convoys, whose own losses had been kept under control by their escorts. In 1942, however, the 'wolf packs' were able to find their way past the escorts and into the heart of convoys to pick and choose from the large number of ships bunched in columns that offered excellent firing opportunities for salvoes of torpedoes. Added to this increased vulnerability of the convoy was the fact that Allied bombing was making no significant impact on the rate of submarine production in Germany, where ever larger numbers of boats were being readied for delivery to a submarine arm ready and willing to expand the 'wolf pack' concept that was now proving so effective.

Such was the Allies' situation in the Atlantic by the end of 1942 that the inter-Allied heads-of-government meeting at Casablanca in French Morocco during January 1943 fixed the defeat of the German submarine threat as the highest single priority, resulting in a further increase in the priority allocated to the construction of anti-submarine escorts and escort carriers in tandem with an increase in the tonnage of bombs aimed at German submarine construction yards.

In January 1943 Dönitz replaced Raeder as commander-in-chief of the German navy, and the emphasis within the navy was now placed even more strongly on the submarine arm *vis-à-vis* the surface force. Between January and March the submarine arm had an average of 116 operational boats available to it, and even though the first two months of the year were lost mostly to appalling weather in the North Atlantic, success continued although at a lesser rate than was achieved in March. In this month better weather returned, and as a direct consequence the submarines sank 108 Allied merchant ships, totalling 627,000 tons, for the loss of a mere 15 of their own number, and in the process reduced the United Kingdom's essential supplies to a reserve of only three months. The major part of the German success came from the interception by a pack of 38 submarines of two convoys in the 'black hole' region of the North Atlantic.

By this time it had become standard practice to attack only one of the three types of merchant shipping operated by the Allies: the type that was constantly attacked was the slow convoy, which was both vulnerable and offered the best type of targets; the two types that remained essentially untouched were the troop convoys, which had very strong escorts, and the independently sailing converted fast liners, which were generally too fast for all but chance submarine interception.

*This is a 'Molch' class midget submarine with two externally carried torpedoes as its armament.*

The tide was about to turn, however, as a result of an increase in Allied anti-submarine capability. This boosted capability came partly from the initiative of a new British commander for the Western Approaches, Admiral Sir Max Horton, who started to implement new tactics based on the use of a free-ranging support force of fast frigates and, whenever possible, an escort carrier, to seek and destroy submarines drawn to the 'magnet' of a convoy that had its own protection in the form of its close escort, and partly from the introduction of larger numbers of modern weapons including very-long-range Consolidated Liberator four-engined aircraft able to range into the 'black hole', shorter-range Vickers Wellington twin-engined aircraft that undertook patrols of the Bay of Biscay with searchlights and/or radar to spot and attack submarines attempting the standard nocturnal departure from their bases on the surface and at high speed, and a combination of improved sensors and weapons so that submarines could be detected more accurately and then taken under attack with a greater chance of securing a 'kill'.

The single episode that most surely revealed the change in the fortune of the German navy's submarine arm was the defence of the ONS-2 convoy between 28 April and 6 May 1943. Comprising 42 merchant ships, the convoy was protected by an escort force under the command of Commander Peter Gretton, one of the men selected by Horton for the implementation of his new tactics. In an epic nine-day battle, the convoy fought its way across the North Atlantic against attacks by 51 U-boats, losing 13 of its number but in the process sinking five of the U-boats, a further two being despatched by aircraft.

This was the turning point in the Battle of the Atlantic, and in May 1943 the Germans lost 38 submarines. Dönitz appreciated at once that this change was no accident, but was really a turning point in the war. Instantly he decided to call off the 'wolf pack' attacks across the breadth of the North Atlantic Ocean, and ordered his submarines to congregate in three areas. These areas comprised the central part of the Atlantic Ocean to the west of the Azores, which was the most vulnerable point in the convoy routes supplying the Allied land effort in the Mediterranean theatre, and two secondary areas that were less afflicted by the attentions of Allied aircraft and anti-submarine escorts, namely the South Atlantic Ocean and the Indian Ocean. In these areas, Dönitz hoped, the submarines would still be able to achieve useful results while he and his staff tried to find a way to revive the U-boat effort.

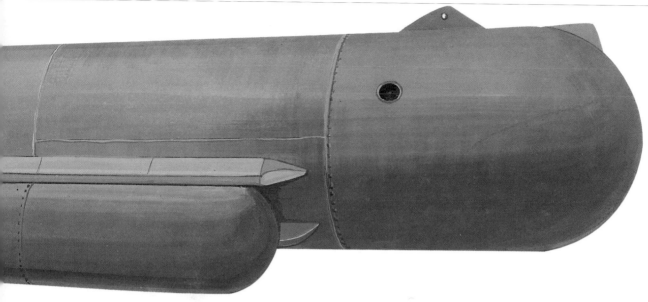

For the remainder of 1943, the tide of battle continued its turn away from the Germans. The submarine arm equipped its boats with more-capable light anti-aircraft defences in an effort to maintain their ability to operate out of western French bases by fighting their way past the British aircraft carriers. The Royal Navy expanded the use of its support groups, and the US Navy chipped in with the 'killer groups' of its 10th Fleet. Each of these 'killer groups' had exceptional freedom of action, and comprised an escort carrier (carrying 24 aircraft) accompanied by several old fleet destroyers or newer destroyer escorts. A further bonus for the Allies was the permission of Portugal in October for the Allies to base anti-submarine aircraft on airfields in the Azores, and this almost closed the 'black hole' in the middle of the Atlantic Ocean.

The success of the Allies is revealed by statistics: between May and September 1943, 3,546 merchant ships crossed the Atlantic in 62 convoys without suffering a single loss to submarine attack; Allied construction of merchant ships exceeded losses by no less than 6 million tons; and between March and November 1943 the German submarine arm lost 204 U-boats. So far as the German losses were concerned, the greatest tragedy for the Germany navy was neither the destruction of submarines nor the loss of their crews, but rather the deaths of large numbers of experienced commanders and their subordinates. With these men went all their wealth of operational experience, and thus the chance of passing the lessons of this experience to trainee crews; the deaths of these officers resulted in high casualty rates during 1944 and 1945.

Dönitz hoped that Germany's position of superiority in the Battle of the Atlantic would be restored by four factors: the *Schnorchel* (snorkel) mast whose use would allow the submarine to run just under the surface on the power of its diesel engines, with only the tip of the mast projecting from the water for the intake of air and for the diesel exhaust; new submarine types such as the Type XXI with a more streamlined hull and conning tower in combination with higher-powered electric motors and higher-capacity batteries for much improved underwater speed and range, and with the possibility of radical upgrade at a later stage by the introduction of the highly advanced Walter propulsion system based on the decomposition of 'Perhydrol' (hydrogen peroxide); new radar for the earlier detection of attacking aircraft and thus a better opportunity to complete a crash dive; and a new type of torpedo that homed acoustically on the sound of the target's engines and propellers.

This quadruple effort was much delayed by Germany's earlier decision to concentrate on the mass production of just a few types of weapon, for the momentum of this effort made it difficult to finalise major changes and introduce them into a production effort that had been widely dispersed to avoid the worst effects of Allied bombers. The problems of introducing new types of boats and weapons were further compounded by Germany's increasing shortage of raw materials, and by the ever-increasing demands of the other armed forces for a greater share of weapons production. In the short term, therefore, the German submariners had to make the best of what was available even though this was now obsolescent as a result of the Allies' greater determination to make the best possible use of developing technologies.

The result was inevitable: in the first three months of 1944, German submarines sank a mere three Allied merchant ships in the North Atlantic, but in the same period suffered the loss of 36 of their own boats to the Allies' rampant anti-submarine capability. This was a disaster for Germany, for during the first six months of 1944, vast numbers of men and vast quantities of matériel crossed the Atlantic to bolster the forces earmarked for the Allied invasion of France.

The technical obsolescence of the majority of his boats, although many had by now been fitted with the snorkelling mast, had persuaded Dönitz temporarily to abandon the Battle of the Atlantic and to husband his resources on a major training programme and preparations for a major intervention against the huge fleet of ships that would be required to transport, maintain and support the Allied invasion. Neither effort achieved useful results, and the success of the Allied invasion, followed by the break-out of the Americans from Normandy to Brittany and western France, deprived Germany of the use of France's Atlantic ports. From the summer of 1944, therefore, the small number of U-boats committed to offensive operations was based in Norwegian waters, and therefore had to make a passage around Britain in order to reach the Atlantic. This unfortunate operational factor was compounded by Allied intervention: bombing was making the construction of new boats (including those produced as prefabricated sections that needed only a short slip time) increasingly difficult, and Allied aerial mining of the Baltic Sea had made training all but impossible.

*The German navy's 1st Submarine Flotilla complete with depot ship.*

*This is a 'Neger' class one-man midget submarine, which was based on a torpedo adapted for operation on the surface (the domed cover was a later addition) with a single underslung 21in (533mm) torpedo as armament. About 200 of this type were placed in service.*

Germany's progressively desperate situation in the autumn of 1944 compelled Dönitz to make one last effort, from November 1944 to April 1945, a period in which the German naval commander hoped that poor weather would hamper the efforts of the Allied anti-submarine forces more than the determination of the German submarine crews. The new tactic devised for this campaign, which was based on the monthly delivery of 27 snorkel-fitted submarines, was to operate initially in the coastal waters around the United Kingdom, where the shallowness of the water had a deleterious effect on the performance of Allied sonar, and then in the Atlantic Ocean. The campaign achieved limited success, for Allied merchant ship losses rose (253,000 tons) and German losses were comparatively light, but the campaign nonetheless posed no real threat to the Allies.

Paradoxically, the German submarine arm reached its peak strength of 463 boats in March 1945, but lacked the crews to operate them against a highly experienced, exceptionally skilled and doggedly determined enemy. It was all too late, however, and in May 1945 Dönitz was compelled, in his capacity as the second Führer of the Third Reich, to agree to an unconditional surrender. In the course of World War II, the German submarine arm had received 1,162 boats and lost 785 of them, in the process sinking 14,300,000 tons of Allied merchant shipping (including 6,840,000 tons in the North Atlantic) as well as 175 Allied warships, the vast majority of them British.

# DIE LUFTWAFFE

Despite a string of early successes as the 'flying artillery' of the German army's Panzer forces in the early days of German *Blitzkrieg* warfare, the Luftwaffe was ultimately a failure as it proved itself incapable of meeting the demands placed upon it. The significance of this failure was fundamental to the ultimate failure of the Third Reich, for air power in World War II was vital to the success of the two other surfaces, and particularly to the success of the land forces, at tactical, operational and strategic levels. At the tactical level, as mentioned above, it provided support for the ground forces over the land battlefield, and thereby increased the success of the ground forces from the tactical to the operational level in Germany's great offensives through Poland, Scandinavia, the Low Countries and France, the Balkans and initially in North Africa and the USSR. In all these cases, the Germans' effective use of their tactical air strength helped the army to produce stunning results.

At the strategic level, however, the Luftwaffe was a failure as first revealed in the Battle of Britain during the summer of 1940: conceived largely for political reasons as a tactical service that could be developed rapidly and economically as an adjunct of the army's operational thinking,

*More than any other German warplane, the Junkers Ju 87 Stuka epitomises the Nazi creed of expansionist warfare, and as such is indelibly linked with the concept of* Blitzkrieg.

the Luftwaffe lacked the aircraft and skills to undertake the strategic role against a determined enemy. This failure became more significant as the war progressed, for the Luftwaffe was then incapable of striking decisive blows against the build-up of the Allied forces in Britain, and therefore of preventing or weakening the blow that eventually fell on German-occupied northern France in June 1944.

By this time, the Luftwaffe had revealed itself to be deficient also in tactical terms as the tide of battle turned and the Germans found themselves fighting a defensive rather than an offensive war: over the Eastern and Italian Fronts the Luftwaffe was unable to ensure the air superiority that would have facilitated the defence of the German ground forces, and this tendency was to become even more pronounced over the Western Front that developed after the Allied invasion of north-west France in June 1944; and over Germany itself, the Luftwaffe fought with enormous dedication and some tactical success, but could not prevent the effective development of the Allied day and night strategic bombing campaign that finally destroyed the energy production capabilities and communications vital for the prosecution of a modern war, and so condemned Germany to inevitable defeat.

All this stemmed from the basic flaw that was built into the Luftwaffe when the Nazi Party came to power in January 1933: the Luftwaffe was created within the specific context of the lightning-fast campaigns that would secure Germany's *Lebensraum* (living space), and could not then be adapted for the creation of strategic-level bombing or operational-level defensive capabilities when the paramount need for these roles was perceived too little and too late. It is therefore arguable that the failure of the Luftwaffe was more responsible for the military defeat of the Third Reich than any other single military factor.

The responsibility for the failure of the Luftwaffe must lie with Adolf Hitler, Hermann Goering and Ernst Udet. All three of these men were

*Although a successful fighter pilot in World War I and initially an able administrator in the creation of the Luftwaffe, Hermann Goering lacked the command skills to ensure that the Luftwaffe was developed along the best longer-term lines, and then committed his service to the wrong type of war in the Battle of Britain.*

responsible for the moulding of the Luftwaffe into a framework that emphasised offensive air operations at the tactical level and with the maximum possible number of aircraft. Hitler was swayed by the propaganda advantages of massed aircraft for domestic as well as international purposes, and could perhaps be excused as a result of his basic lack of knowledge of air warfare except for the fact that he interfered constantly. There is less excuse for Goering and Udet, who were respectively the air minister and Luftwaffe's commander-in-chief, and the head of design and procurement during the Luftwaffe's formative years. Both men had been air aces in World War I (Udet ranking second only to the great Rittmeister Manfred, Freiherr von Richthofen), but in the mid- and late 1930s they were more interested in increasing their positions of authority within the German hierarchy than with objective planning for an air force that common sense demanded should at least possess a defensive capability to match its offensive power.

Although capable pilots in their time, both Goering and Udet were woefully ignorant of the rapidly developing technology that was conditioning the development of air power during the 1930s, while the need of both men to maintain a moral and political ascendancy over potential rivals would not have permitted them to seek advice.

Udet did finally perceive the desperate situation to which his lack of perception had brought the Luftwaffe by late 1941, and committed suicide. His successor was Erhard Milch, who was already Goering's deputy and, although placed relatively low in the pecking order of the Nazi hierarchy, had the skills to appreciate what was required. It was too late to affect the outcome of the war in the air, but Milch must be credited for the development and introduction of the warplanes with which the Luftwaffe fought so determinedly if ultimately so unsuccessfully between 1943 and 1945.

Two other senior officers of the Luftwaffe also deserve mention at this time. The first of these was Generalleutnant Walther Wever, who was the

*At the beginning of World War II, Luftwaffe aircrew were highly capable in the type of warfare for which they had been trained, but lacked adequate reserves and the right type of training infrastructure for the campaigns of attrition that would eventually whittle them away.*

new Luftwaffe's first chief-of-staff. Somewhat rarely among his contemporaries, Wever realised the importance of developing a strategic bombing capability, and indeed started the process that might have led the Luftwaffe into becoming a more balanced air force, but he was killed in an air accident in 1936. Wever was succeeded by Generalleutnant Hans Jeschonnek, who was a devotee of tactical air power but so single-minded that virtually no discussion of strategic air power was possible until his departure from office in 1943, by which time it was too late for any change in the Luftwaffe's structure.

Almost without exception, other senior Luftwaffe commanders had been army officers before their transfer to the Luftwaffe and were therefore basically inclined to the notion of a tactical air force matched to the requirements of army support. It was only at the middle- and low-ranking command levels that 'true airmen' were to be encountered: men such as Adolf Galland and Josef Kammhuber who had joined the Luftwaffe in its earliest days and rose to senior, but not the most senior, command levels during the middle and later stages of World War II.

Given its operational subordination to the army, the Luftwaffe was based on the army in organisational terms. The largest Luftwaffe formation was the *Luftflotte* (air fleet) that corresponded to the army group, and this was a temporary grouping of subordinate formations optimised for the relevant operational task, and capable of expansion or contraction in organisational and geographical terms to suit changing tasks. Throughout most of World War II there were four *Luftflotten*, although three more were added in 1944 to cater for the expansion (or perhaps fragmentation) of Luftwaffe operations in line with those of the ever-changing army groups.

Next down the Luftwaffe's table of organisation was the *Fliegerkorps* (flying corps), which was another formation of varying size and composition, although in the later stages of the war there were a very few *Jagdkorps* (fighter corps) for specialised tasks. Each *Luftflotte* was composed of two or more *Fliegerkorps*, whose main constituent element was the

*Geschwader* (group) that was the Luftwaffe's largest homogeneous unit. In the early part of the war the most important types of *Geschwader*, which generally had between 90 and 120 aircraft, were the *Jagdgeschwadern* (fighter groups), *Kampfgeschwadern* (bomber groups), *Stukageschwadern* (dive-bomber groups) and *Zerstörergeschwadern* (heavy fighter groups). Each *Geschwader* was composed of three *Gruppen* (wings) each of between 30 and 40 aircraft provided by the three subordinate *Staffeln* (squadrons) of 10 to 15 aircraft each.

Administrative support for the *Luftflotten* and their subordinate formations and units was provided by the *Luftgaue* (air regions), which were territorially based and therefore fixed in their capabilities. This again mirrored the administrative system operated by the army, but was perhaps less appropriate in this instance as it is arguable that the *Luftgaue* should perhaps have been under the control of the army rather than the *Luftflotten* that were themselves allocated to army groups. This would have removed a certain degree of administrative duplication, but was not permitted by Goering for reasons of Luftwaffe pride and, in the early part of the

*Left and below: The Heinkel He 111 was Germany's best and most numerous medium bomber of the period early in World War II, but was forced to fly on into obsolescence for lack of an adequate replacement.*

Luftwaffe's development, his belief that the army was not fully committed to Nazi party ideals.

However, this basic organisation was well suited to the Luftwaffe in its originally conceived task of tactical air support for the army in *Blitzkrieg* operations, but less well suited to the longer-term development of the air force, when separate fighter and bomber commands would have been a decided asset in allowing the concentration of forces for specific tasks such as the Battle of Britain in the summer of 1940, the securing and maintenance of air superiority over key sectors of the Eastern Front in the period between 1942 and 1944, and the air defence of Germany between 1943 and 1945.

It is worth noting that the Luftwaffe also included high-quality ground forces, for the German anti-aircraft and airborne forces arms were part of the Luftwaffe rather than the army. Both these branches of the Luftwaffe were organised along army lines, from corps down to platoon, and were highly capable organisations that at times played a decisive part in German operations: the *Fliegerabwehrkanone* (anti-aircraft gun) arm was well equipped and well trained, and with its three variants of 88mm (3.465in) Flak gun had one of World War II's most capable weapons that had been designed for the anti-aircraft role but also proved itself an excellent anti-tank weapon; while the *Fallschirmjäger* (airborne) arm comprised high-quality troops, with good weapons and first-class fighting morale, who paved the way for the German ground advances through the Low Countries in May 1940, and took Crete in May 1941, and thereafter served as high-quality ground forces who acquired a fearsome reputation for defensive capability, exemplified at the Battle of Monte Cassino in the spring of 1944.

The fighting for Crete was both the making and undoing of the Luftwaffe's airborne arm, for the campaign resulted in very considerable losses of men and aircraft, but also revealed the sterling fighting qualities of the German paratrooper, especially under adverse operational conditions. The former fact was largely responsible for Hitler's decision that the airborne arm should not again be used in the airborne role, which effectively ruled out the planned German and Italian airborne assault on Malta, the British island bastion whose capture by Axis forces might have altered the balance of power in the Mediterranean at a decisive moment, while the latter fact was responsible for the airborne arm's survival as an elite formation that was eventually expanded to 10 divisions with almost 250,000 men.

The Luftwaffe's other ground troops were the high-grade Hermann Goering Regiment that was later expanded into a Panzer division and eventually into a parachute corps, and the lower-grade Luftwaffe field divisions that were used mainly for rear-area security and other second-line tasks.

Planned for the offensive role in support of the army, the Luftwaffe was initially equipped with adequate numbers of the right types of aircraft. This arrangement sufficed until mid-1940, for up to this time the Luftwaffe was called upon in its originally conceived role in short-term campaigns of aggression. Then the Luftwaffe was forced by the evolving nature of World War II to embark upon a number of other tasks, and was immediately found wanting in terms of numbers and types of warplane. Numbers of warplanes were inadequate because a moderately low but steady rate of production had been planned around the concept of a series of short campaigns in which the aircraft lost in one campaign would be replaced in the interval before the launching of the next. Types of warplane were found lacking for the twin reasons that confidence in total success in a very short time had led both to the curtailment of longer-term planning and development (resulting in a measure of warplane obsolescence that could be mitigated only by a process of developing current types to the ultimate degree), and to a concentration on warplanes tailored exactly to current requirements without adequate consideration of how these requirements might alter if the *Blitzkrieg* concept was no longer dominant.

This failure in planning meant that the Luftwaffe was unable to meet its later requirements for strategic bombers and defensive fighters. Although this failure was embodied in the wrong grand strategic plan it had been given, it was compounded by Adolf Hitler's overwhelming adherence to the concept of offensive operations. Even in 1944, for example, when Germany was in no position to launch anything more than tactical offensive operations, Luftwaffe warplane development and procurement were hampered by the German leader's insistence that there should be no such thing as a dedicated defensive fighter but only fighter-bombers able to deliver significant offensive loads.

This emphasis on the ability to deliver a useful offensive load also conditioned the Luftwaffe's main bomb-carriers for the *Blitzkrieg* role, which were the medium bomber and the dive-bomber. The medium bomber was conceived as a relatively small type with a high power-to-weight ratio for good performance and agility. These parameters resulted in medium bombers able to deliver medium-size bomb loads over short-to-medium ranges with a good chance of avoiding or outflying the fighter opposition, but made it impossible for the resulting warplanes to be developed for the strategic role in terms of either bomb load or range.

The first of these bombers was the Dornier Do 17, generally known to the British as the 'Flying Pencil' for its very slim fuselage. The type could carry a bomb load of 2,205lb (1,000kg) and was both fast and manoeuvrable, especially at low level, by the standards of 1939 but then proved to be disastrously vulnerable to rear attack during the Battle of Britain, when the higher performance of their fighters gave British pilots the opportunity to select this attack angle. Further development of the Do 17, which was produced only in modest numbers, produced the Do 215 with greater power for higher performance and thus greater survivability, and the Do 217 that was an enlarged and strengthened derivative capable of carrying an 8,818lb (4,000kg) bomb load for use in semi-diving attacks. The Do 215 and Do 217 were also made only in modest numbers, and were used mainly in the anti-shipping role.

Numerically more important was the Heinkel He 111, which was the Luftwaffe's medium bomber mainstay throughout World War II even though it was obsolescent by 1940 and totally obsolete by 1942. In its definitive He 111H-16 version the bomber could deliver 4,409lb (2,000kg) of bombs and was, in its heyday, a capable type that was versatile and easy to handle. From mid-1943 the type was less important as its obsolescence and indifferent defensive armament rendered it vulnerable to interception and destruction even in secondary theatres, but the type remained in service in more specialised roles until the end of the war.

The most important bomber used by the Luftwaffe throughout World War II was the Junkers Ju 88, which has a claim against the de Havilland Mosquito to having been the most versatile warplane of World War II if not of all time. Deliveries amounted to about 15,000 aircraft of all types

*This partial cut-away illustration highlights the defensive features of the Heinkel He 111, which was sadly lacking in forward-hemisphere defensive capability.*

*The Heinkel He 111Z was a specialised development of the He 111H in which two He 111H airframes were connected by a new centre section carrying a fifth engine. The type's task was the towing of very large gliders such as the Messerschmitt Me 321, and only a few of the type were completed.*

including reconnaissance, night fighting and ground-attack. The Ju 88 could carry a bomb load of 4,409lb (2,000kg) over a tactically useful range at high speed, and its combination of strength and agility gave it a good measure of survivability against Allied fighter attack.

The development of the Ju 88 exemplifies the effect of the Luftwaffe's demand for optimisation in the tactical bombing role. As originally conceived, the Ju 88 would have been able to deliver 4,409lb (2,000kg) of bombs over a radius of 1,000 miles (1,610km) at a speed of more than 300mph (485km/h). Udet decided, however, that the Ju 88 should also possess a dive-bombing capability as a means of enhancing its effect in the tactical role by maximising the accuracy of its bomb delivery, and the need to provide air brakes and strengthen the airframe for the dive-bombing role added considerably to weight and therefore eroded performance in terms of speed and tactical radius. Yet such was the demand for the new type, despite its reduced performance, that it was rushed into production before its development had been successfully completed, with the result that early production and use were bedevilled by stoppages and problems as faults were rectified, and it was 1943 before the type was fully effective.

All three of these basic medium bomber types suffered from two main tactical failings, namely the concentration of the crew in the forward fuselage and the limited nature of the defensive armament, which was based on manually operated single machine guns rather than turreted weapons. The concentration of the crew was thought to offer the psychological advantage of mutual support and interoperability, and had the additional advantage of reducing demands on airframe size and therefore structure weight: operations later revealed that it also increased the vulnerability of the crew to concentrated fire; it was virtually impossible to increase the weight of defensive fire except by the addition of more single or twin machine guns, almost invariably in otherwise unused corners of the crew compartment that could not effectively carry more gunners, and demanded that the current crew members move from one position to another to tackle multiple attackers or even to track a single fighter. Greater fuselage size would therefore have paid considerable dividends in the ability to carry a larger crew and the installation of turreted armament when such items became advisable for the concentration of heavier fire in certain vulnerable sectors.

Such was the emphasis on these bombers, however, that design and development of successor bombers was either cancelled or shifted to a lower priority. In 1938 it had been decided that the Ju 88 should become the Luftwaffe's standard bomber, so it was 1939 before the Luftwaffe came to the conclusion that a new 'Bomber B' type should be developed for service as the air force's standard bomber from 1942. The type selected for development in this role was the Junkers Ju 288, a derivative of the concepts already embodied in the Ju 88, but progress with this new type was also bedevilled by Udet's insistence on the incorporation of a dive-bombing capability. The type's estimated capabilities would have provided a modest strategic facility, but at the end of 1941 Milch, as Udet's successor, realised that delays and other problems would postpone the service debut of the Ju 288 until 1944, and therefore he ordered the further development of the Ju 88 in its improved forms and also as the Ju 188, a superior type of which just over 1,000 were delivered for service from May 1943. Continued problems with the Ju 288 resulted in the type being cancelled in June 1943, leaving the Luftwaffe with a complete absence of a large-scale medium bomber capability and also with no realistic facility in the strategic role.

Specialised strategic bombers were being planned by Wever before his death in June 1936, but further work on such four-engined types was then cancelled as it was considered more expedient to concentrate on single- and twin-engined machines, as the propaganda value of two twin-engined bombers was thought to be considerably greater than that of a single four-engined machine.

Limited work continued on two such types, the Dornier Do 19 and the Junkers Ju 89, within the context of the 'Ural Bomber' programme designed to provide the Luftwaffe with the ability to strike at the Soviet industrial regions to the east of the Ural Mountains, but Goering finally cancelled the programme on the grounds that two or even three twin-engined bombers could result from the resources required to complete just one four-engined bomber, and because Hitler would 'never ask me how big our bombers are, but how many we have': the Nazi leader's penchant for quantity rather than quality was to have a serious long-term effect on Germany's ability to wage a protracted war.

Even though a dedicated strategic bomber was therefore ruled out, the Luftwaffe had no objection to a heavy bombing capability as long as this could be combined with a dive-bombing capability. The two requirements were in effect incompatible, but work began on the interesting Heinkel He 177 Greif, with four engines coupled into two pairs to drive two large propellers. An enormous quantity of time and resources was expended on this type – which was never satisfactory as a result of its powerplant, whose tendency to ignite resulted in the aeroplane's 'flying firework' nickname – and the need to incorporate a dive-bombing capability, and even Goering

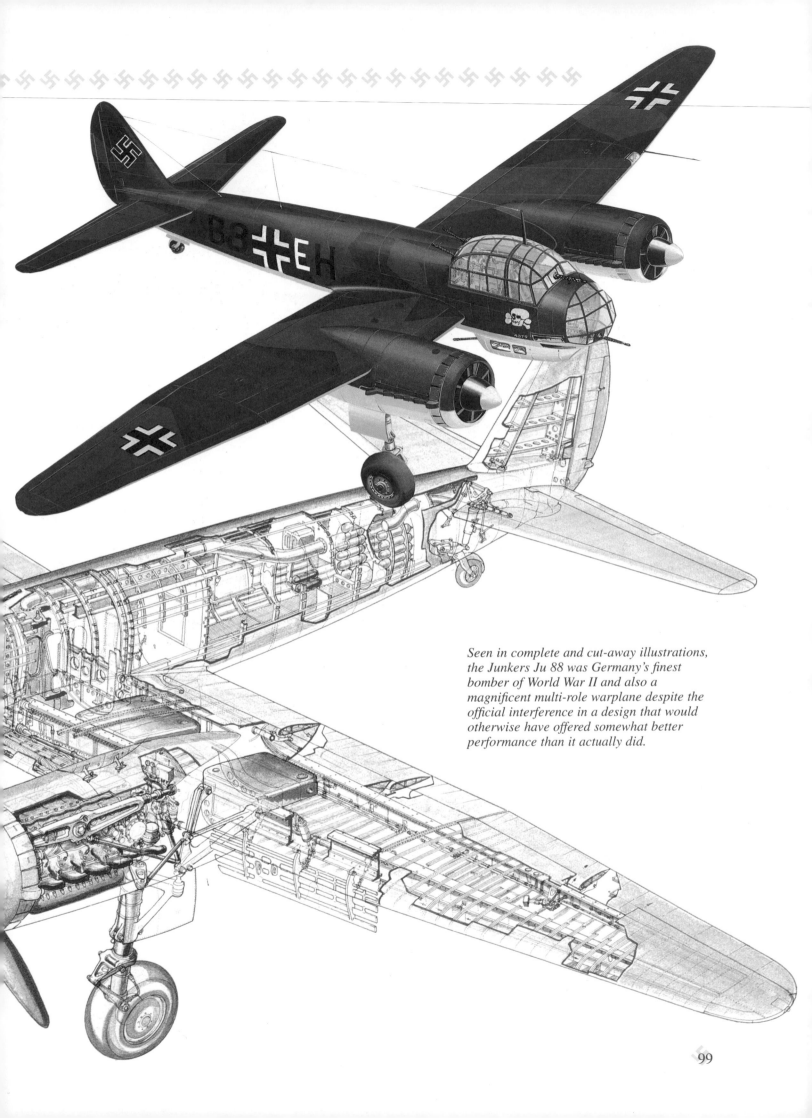

Seen in complete and cut-away illustrations, the Junkers Ju 88 was Germany's finest bomber of World War II and also a magnificent multi-role warplane despite the official interference in a design that would otherwise have offered somewhat better performance than it actually did.

finally remarked that 'It is straightforward idiocy to ask of a four-engined bomber that it should dive.'

At the lower end of the size and technology spectrum, the Luftwaffe's primary bomb carrier was the Junkers Ju 87, universally known as the Stuka as an abbreviation of its German name *Sturzkampfflugzeug* (dive-bomber). The Stuka has become virtually synonymous with the *Blitzkrieg* for it was this type, with its cranked wing, stooping attack method and morale-devastating 'Jericho trumpet' sirens on the main units of its fixed landing gear, that opened the way for the Panzer divisions by blasting the enemy's front-line defences and then roaming into the enemy's rear areas to devastate lines of communication, reinforcement assembly areas, fuel and ammunition dumps, command centres, and, most vividly remembered of all, hapless columns of refugees whose panic further hindered the efforts of Germany's enemies to mount a cohesive defence. The Ju 87 was technically obsolescent even before the outbreak of World War II, but absence of any effective fighter or anti-aircraft artillery opposition gave it *carte blanche* to secure decisive results in the Polish and North-West European campaigns. It was only when the type was committed against a first-class fighter defence in the Battle of Britain that the limitations of the Stuka were revealed, and the type's very heavy losses in just a few engagements led to its rapid withdrawal from the battle, thereby denying the Luftwaffe the ability to inflict decisive point damage on targets such as radar stations.

Further successes followed the type's use against negligible opposition in the Balkans and in the first stages of the Soviet campaigns, but thereafter the Stuka was gradually relegated to the ground-attack role with cannon and light bombs, and even then had to operate mostly at night even against the limited air defence that the USSR was able to offer up to mid-1943. There was no successor to the Ju 87, however, the planned Messerschmitt Me 210 having suffered apparently intractable development problems, so

*Top: The Junkers Ju 86, seen here in bomber form, was a type planned for construction in parallel civil and military forms, but was built almost exclusively for military roles including, in its final forms, photo-reconnaissance at very high altitudes.*

the Ju 87 was retained in production until 1944, by which time it was totally obsolete.

The Ju 87 series was finally replaced not by one type, but by three types of machine in the form of specialised variants of the Focke-Wulf Fw 190 single-engined fighter, the Messerschmitt Me 410 twin-engined multi-role warplane that was developed from the unsuccessful Me 210, and the Henschel Hs 129 twin-engined anti-tank warplane. The Hs 129 was very heavily armoured and carried highly potent armament, but was rendered virtually useless by the pilot's very poor fields of vision and by the lack of a sufficiently powerful powerplant, which reduced performance to an unacceptable degree and also inhibited pilots from trying to manoeuvre at low level for fear of running out of vital airspeed and altitude.

Given the fact that it was the number and capabilities of Allied and Soviet tanks, backed by other armoured fighting vehicles and highly mobile artillery, that signalled the defeat of the German army from 1943, the Luftwaffe's lack of an effective anti-armour warplane was a failing of monumental proportions that related directly to Germany's final defeat.

Whilst the bomber, of both the level and dive types, was considered to be

**Below:** *Seen in anti-tank form, the Ju 87 was at best obsolescent by 1940 but soldiered on in development and production for lack of an effective successor.*

the Luftwaffe's primary weapon in the period up to the middle of 1942, the same was not true of the fighter. Considerable attention was given to the need to protect Germany from the attentions of Allied bombers, but such a capability was thought to be provided by modest numbers of older fighters and a leavening of more modern machines. The real role of the modern fighter was therefore seen as being tactical in nature, as protection for the German bombers operating over and beyond the front line, and as a defence against enemy air attack on the German army's front-line and rear-area positions. This situation is typified by production figures for 1940, the first full year of World War II: in these 12 months German industry delivered 10,247 aircraft, and of these only 2,746 were fighters by comparison with 3,455 bombers. By 1942, when the need for a larger proportion of fighters was at last being appreciated, the production totals for bombers and fighters were essentially similar (5,586 bombers and 5,518 fighters); it was only in 1943 that fighter production began to exceed that of bombers by any appreciable degree: Milch later opined that the Luftwaffe's most glaring error had been the '140,000 unbuilt fighter aircraft'.

Although there were faults in the Luftwaffe's perception of the fighter's role and in the number of such aircraft that were produced in the period up to 1943, there was nothing inexpedient with the service's standard fighter at the beginning of World War II, the Messerschmitt Bf 109, which was currently in service in its Bf 109D and Bf 109E variants. A pioneering single-engined fighter of the 'modern' type, with a stressed-skin metal construction and a cantilever low-wing configuration that included features such as an enclosed cockpit, tailwheel landing gear with fully retractable main unit, a flapped wing, and provision for cannon armament, the Bf 109 was the equal of any fighter in the world, and with its fuel-injected Daimler-Benz DB 601 inverted-Vee engine was probably the tactical superior of even the Supermarine Spitfire with its normally carburetted Rolls-Royce Merlin Vee piston engine.

Such was the prowess of the Bf 109, which was evaluated operationally during the Spanish Civil War, that the Luftwaffe believed that development of a second-generation 'modern' fighter was not a matter of any great

*In general, the Germans lacked the abilities of the Soviets to keep their aircraft flying under very severe winter conditions, even after they introduced cumbersome but inefficient warming systems such as that seen here with a Junkers Ju 88 fast bomber.*

*The Dornier Do 17 and Do 215 series of medium bombers offered good performance by the standards prevalent in the early stages of World War II, but carried only a modest bomb load and were deficient in defensive capabilities.*

urgency – after all, it was believed that Germany would have secured all her objectives by 1941 at the latest, when the superiority of the Bf 109 would still be unchallenged. Yet by 1940 it was clear that the war would indeed last beyond 1941, and development of more advanced fighters was accelerated even as improved versions of the Bf 109 were planned and placed in production and service. The Bf 109E was therefore followed by the Bf 109F that was generally reckoned to have marked the high point of the Bf 109's development, for greater power was allied with a number of individually small but collectively important structural and aerodynamic enhancements to produce a fighter that had high performance and excellent handling

*The Henschel Hs 129 was conceived as a very powerful tank-killing warplane that would be relatively invulnerable to anti-aircraft fire up to medium calibres, but was so heavy and underpowered that performance was very low. The pilot also had wholly inadequate fields of vision from his very cramped cockpit.*

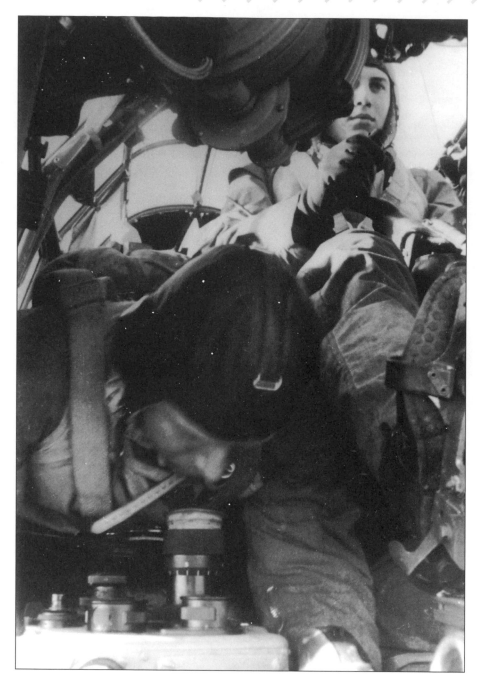

characteristics. Operational pilots complained, however, because firepower was actually reduced in this model, and the Bf 109F was soon followed by the Bf 109G that became the definitive model with still greater power and considerably heavier armament that was often supplemented by items added as factory- or field-installed kits. The Bf 109G was produced in larger numbers than any other Bf 109 variant and had a number of superb exponents among Germany's highest-scoring air aces, but was without doubt a poorer flying machine than its predecessors even though outright performance had been improved by the adoption of the higher-powered DB 605 engine. The only other major model was the Bf 109K with further 'tweakings' of the design for enhancement of the Bf 109G's capabilities, but the Bf 109K was produced only in modest numbers.

Good as the Bf 109 series was in overall warplane terms, especially in performance (resulting from the marriage of a high-powered engine with a small airframe), agility and combination of high climb rate and angle, it had

*The extensive glazing of the forward crew compartment typical of German bombers offered good fields of vision but also left the crew members very vulnerable to surface-to-air as well as air-to-air fire.*

104

*The best fighter available to the Luftwaffe in the first part of World War II was the Messerschmitt Bf 109E, seen here in the form of an aeroplane of Jagdgeschwader 26 'Schlageter', more specifically the 9.Staffel of the Geschwader's III Gruppe.*

two major failings so far as the Luftwaffe was concerned. The first of these was apparent from the beginning of the type's career, and was the general lack of strength in the main landing gear units, which were also of tactically limiting narrow track as they retracted outwards into the undersurfaces of the wing rather than inwards to the underside of the wing roots or fuselage. The second failing became clear only as the war progressed, and was a lack of range/endurance resulting from the fact that the type had been planned within the context of *Blitzkrieg*, which demanded nothing more than short-range endurance. In the Battle of Britain, however, longer range was required and the Bf 109E was found wanting in this respect. Nothing major could be achieved in the way of extending the Bf 109E's range and endurance in the short term, but later variants had their range and endurance boosted by provision for drop tanks of the type that became increasingly common in World War II as a means of supplementing a fighter's internal fuel capacity.

It was only from July 1941 that the Bf 109 was complemented by a more advanced fighter, the superb Focke-Wulf Fw 190 that gave the British a

considerable shock when it appeared and gained an immediate superiority over their latest fighter, the Spitfire Mk V. Fortunately for the British, however, the Fw 190A was initially produced in small numbers, partially as a result of engine reliability problems, and the type made its debut over the Eastern Front only in September 1942. Once the type's initial problems had been overcome, deliveries accelerated rapidly, allowing delivery of some 20,000 aircraft by the end of the war, in comparison to more than 30,000 of the Bf 109 series. By July 1944, monthly deliveries of the Bf 109 and Fw 190 were each in excess of 1,000 aircraft.

The Fw 190 was unusual among Western European fighters of its time in being powered by an air-cooled radial engine rather than a liquid-cooled Vee engine, but the larger frontal area of this type of powerplant was offset by the very neat installation of a low-drag cowling and by the high power-to-weight ratio offered by its avoidance of heavy coolant liquid, its radiator and all the associated plumbing. The Fw 190 therefore provided first-class agility together with very high performance and potent firepower from the beginning of its career, and was then developed in both radial- and Vee-engined forms, the latter retaining a radial-engined appearance as a result of the use of an annular radiator in the Fw 190D 'long-nose' series with the Junkers Jumo 213 engine. The Fw 190 was a considerably more versatile warplane than the Bf 109, and was produced in specialised variants for the interceptor, fighter-bomber, ground-attack, reconnaissance and torpedo attack roles.

Both the Bf 109 and Fw 190 could have been supplemented from 1943 and possibly replaced from 1944 by an altogether superior breed of warplane, the Messerschmitt Me 262 with a turbojet- rather than piston-

*Left: This is a Messerschmitt Bf 109E of II Gruppe of Jagdgeschwader 3 'Udet'.*

*Below: This piggyback combination of a Messerschmitt Bf 109 fighter above a DFS 230 glider was developed experimentally during 1942-43 in an effort to find an effective method of delivering the assault glider over a considerable range without the use of a multi-engined tug aeroplane. The piggyback combination could take-off, climb and cruise on the power of the fighter's engine, and the glider was released only when within gliding range of its objective.*

engined powerplant. Ultimately the type entered moderately large-scale service only in the middle of 1944, partially as a result of the difficulties in developing the entirely novel engines to an acceptable level of reliability, but also because of the interference of Nazi party functionaries including Hitler himself, who initially refused to sanction the further development of the type (as it would interfere with bomber development and production) and then demanded that the type be produced only if it could be adapted as a high-speed bomber.

Finally the type did enter production, with a large measure of subterfuge in an effort to avoid Hitler's strictures, and revealed its capabilities in its first month of operation. By this time, the Allies had total air superiority, yet a force of only twenty-five Me 262 fighters was able to shoot down 50 Allied bombers. With a speed of 540mph (870km/h), when Allied fighters were limited to a maximum of about 425mph (685km/h), and armed with four 30mm cannon against most Allied fighters' six 0.5in (12.7mm) machine guns, four 20mm cannon, or two 20mm cannon and a number of machine guns, the Me 262 was a generation ahead of all the Allied fighters including their sole turbojet-powered type, the Gloster Meteor, that was little more than a piston-engined fighter redesigned for turbojet power and therefore wholly inferior to the Me 262. Production of the Me 262 totalled just under 1,300 by the end of World War II, and their success was ultimately prevented only by shortages of fuel and continuing engine problems.

The Germans' other main fighter of the World War II period was the Messerschmitt Bf 110, a twin-engined warplane contemporary with the Bf 109. There was considerable enthusiasm from several European nations as well as the USA and Japan during the mid-1930s for a twin-engined heavy fighter to complement their primary forces of single-engined light fighters optimised for the interception role. The twin-engined fighter was seen as offering a multi-role capability through its carriage of a two- or three-man

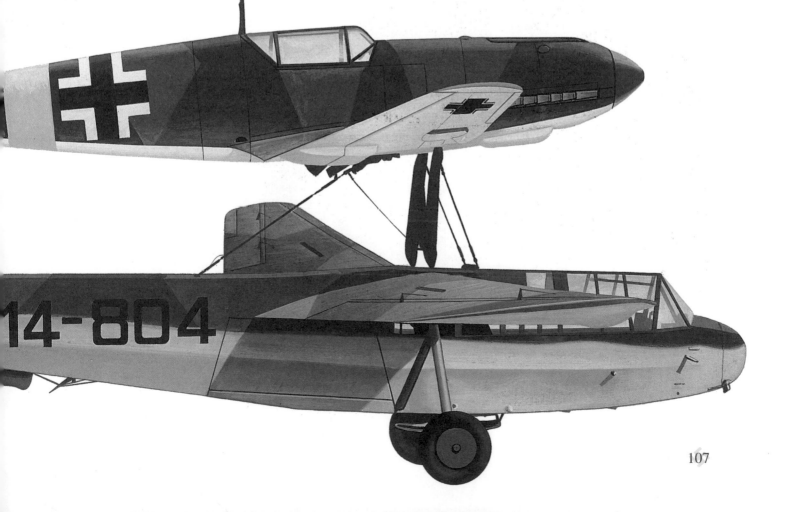

*Top: Seen here with one large bomb under the fuselage and two drop tanks under the wing, the Focke-Wulf Fw 190A was developed as a fighter but was soon adapted for a host of other roles including the fighter-bomber and ground-attack tasks.*

*Left: The cockpit of the Focke-Wulf Fw 190 was excellently planned along ergonomic lines, and also offered the pilot very good fields of vision.*

crew (one man operating a trainable machine gun for rearward defence), heavy fixed armament that could be supplemented by externally carried bombs, high speed as a result of its twin-engined powerplant, and considerable range as a result of the large quantity of fuel that could be carried in the comparatively capacious airframe. The multi-role concept was attractive by the fact that it seemed to offer a cost-effective solution to several tactical needs, and the Germans saw in the type the potential for a

*Zerstörer* (destroyer) that could serve as an escort for Germany's bomber forces while also offering the capability for long-range reconnaissance and interception of Allied bombers.

In most respects the Bf 110 met its requirements, but like all other twin-engined heavy fighters it ultimately failed as a result of the primary limitation inherent in its concept: as a twin-engined warplane it was larger and heavier than the single-engined fighters with which it was confronted and, while this permitted the installation of heavy armament, it also made the heavy fighter less nimble than its opponents, which could therefore choose the opportunity to enter or break off combat. Consequently, the Bf 110 force suffered very heavy casualties in the Battle of Britain, and the Germans decided to concentrate further development of this type on its fighter-bomber, shipping escort and attack, and reconnaissance variants.

**Left:** *The BMW 801 engine, which was the original powerplant for the Focke-Wulf Fw 190 series, was a two-row radial engine offering considerable reliability and fuel economy with a high power-to-weight ratio.*

**Below:** *Arguably the finest fighter operated by the Luftwaffe in World War II, the Focke-Wulf Fw 190 was potently armed and very rugged, offered very good levels of performance and, just as importantly, was also a pilot's aeroplane with powerful yet well-balanced controls.*

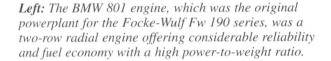

A further lease of life was provided to the Bf 110 by the British decision to concentrate its growing strategic bomber effort in night operations to avoid the heavy losses suffered during daytime bomber raids. The Germans were therefore faced with the need for a larger and more sophisticated force of night fighters to tackle this British threat. Single-engined fighters were not suitable for nocturnal operations, and also lacked the volume for the incorporation of radar (together with its operator) when this became available, but the Bf 110 was well suited to this task albeit with slight loss of performance as a result of the weight of the radar equipment and the drag of its antenna array. The Bf 110 remained in service up to the end of World War II in a number of steadily improved night fighter models, but was later supplemented by versions of the Ju 88 multi-role warplane and, later still, by the Heinkel He 219 twin-engined night fighter. The He 219 was, without doubt, one of the finest warplanes of World War II in terms of its excellent performance despite the incorporation of heavy armament, radar and pioneering ejector seats. Production of the Bf 110 lasted to March 1945 and totalled 6,050 aircraft.

*Captured examples of enemy aircraft were always very useful for an assessment of their overall capabilities and also, as revealed here, for examination by aircrews as an aid to identification in the air. This Focke-Wulf Fw 190 captured by the British is being examined by American aircrews.*

**Right:** *There can be little denial of the fact that the Messerschmitt Me 262 turbojet-powered fighter was a most capable fighter to see extensive service in World War II.*

*One of the roles in which the highly versatile Junkers Ju 88 proved most successful was that of night fighter, in which the weighty and 'draggy' antennae of the typical German radar installation could be carried without an undue loss of performance.*

In addition to the Luftwaffe's primary warplane types, there were a number of other significant machines including the twin-engined Arado Ar 234 Blitz pioneering turbojet-powered bomber and reconnaissance aeroplane, the single-engined Fieseler Fi 156 Storch STOL type for the battlefield reconnaissance and liaison roles, the four-engined Focke-Wulf Fw 200 Condor derivative of a pre-war airliner for the maritime reconnaissance and anti-shipping roles, the three-engined Junkers Ju 52/3m tactical transport and glider tug, and the Messerschmitt Me 163 Komet point interceptor with a single liquid-propellant rocket motor for very high speed and a phenomenal rate of climb at the expense of exceptionally low-powered endurance and extreme danger as it landed on an extending skid.

A factor that must certainly be taken into account in any consideration of the performance of the German fighter forces in World War II is the skill of German fighter pilots, who proved themselves superior to those of the Allies and the Soviets. By generally accepted standards, which define an 'ace' (or *Experte* in German terms) as any pilot who has achieved five or more aerial victories, the Germans had more than 5,000 aces in World War II. It is often suggested that German pilots were able to accumulate large scores for a number of reasons: that they had often learned their skills in the Spanish Civil War; that they were operating largely over their own territory (which usually allowed for the recovery of any pilot who had to take to his parachute); that they flew very many more missions than their opponents as there was no German system of tours (on completion of which the pilot was rotated to an administrative or training appointment); and that over the Eastern Front they were faced by a virtually limitless number of targets that represented easy prey, as the Soviet training system created only second-rate pilots.

The first factor is generally true of the greatest aces of the period early in the war, when both direct and indirect experience was used to boost the overall tactical skills of German fighter pilots. The second factor is true only in the later stages of the war when Germany was wholly on the defensive, for in the first stages of World War II German pilots almost invariably operated over enemy territory in pursuit of their offensive goals. The third factor is certainly true, for after reaching the front, German pilots generally remained there except for periods of leave or after having been wounded. The fourth factor is partially true, as Soviet warplanes flown by indifferent pilots were indeed available as potential targets in vast numbers up to the end

*One of the most advanced warplanes to see service in World War II, the Arado Ar 234 Blitz was a turbojet-powered reconnaissance bomber which lacked fuselage volume for any bomb load, which was therefore carried externally.*

of 1942. Thereafter the number of Soviet aircraft increased, and so did the skills of their pilots after the lessons of the first 18 months of air warfare over the Eastern Front had been digested and their implications put to practical use in the training of new pilots with better flying and tactical skills.

Whatever the reasons, it was certainly true that German pilots believed that the Allied air forces were equipped until the later stages of the war with warplanes that were generally superior to those of the Soviet air force, and flown by pilots with skills superior to their own. Even so, the leading British ace of the Battle of Britain scored only half the number of kills scored by the three leading German aces of the period, namely Helmuth Wick, Werner Mölders and Adolf Galland, despite the fact that the Germans were operating a long way from home and the British had by far the larger number of targets to engage.

This tendency is perhaps best exemplified by Hauptmann Hans Joachim Marseille, Germany's highest-scoring ace against the Allies. Operating over North Africa, Marseille shot down no fewer than 158 Allied aircraft (including 17 in one day), 57 of them in the last month before his death in September 1942 after an engine failure. This victory total was achieved in 482 sorties, and there can be no doubt that this gifted aerial fighter secured his amazing success through a combination of exceptional piloting and gunnery skills.

Much the same can be said of the highest scoring ace of all time, Major Erich Hartmann, who arrived on the Eastern Front in October 1942, and by the summer of 1943 had achieved results (30 victories) that were indifferent by the standards of the theatre. By the end of World War II, however,

*Above right and below: The Junkers Ju 52/3m was the Luftwaffe's transport and airborne forces aeroplane throughout World War II despite the fact that the type was obsolete from 1940 onward.*

Hartmann was credited with an astounding 352 victories in some 1,400 sorties as a pilot of Jagdgeschwader 52, the Luftwaffe's highest-scoring fighter unit with some 11,000 credited victories. Like Marseille, Hartmann was an excellent pilot and a superb aerial shot, and his career was all the more remarkable for the fact that he was shot down on several occasions (once being taken prisoner by the Soviets, but subsequently escaping).

The only other ace to score more than 300 victories was Major Gerhard Barkhorn with 301 'kills' in 1,104 sorties, and other leading *Experten* were Major Günther Rall (275 victories), Oberleutnant Otto Kittel (267 victories in only 583 sorties), and Major Walther Novotny (250 victories including 167 in a mere four months). The highest victory/sortie rate was secured by Major Wilhelm Batz, who shot down 237 aircraft in only 455 sorties. These men were aces of the Eastern Front, and perhaps just as great was Oberstleutnant Heinrich Bär, who shot down 124 Allied aircraft before being transferred to the Eastern Front, where he dispatched 96 Soviet warplanes.

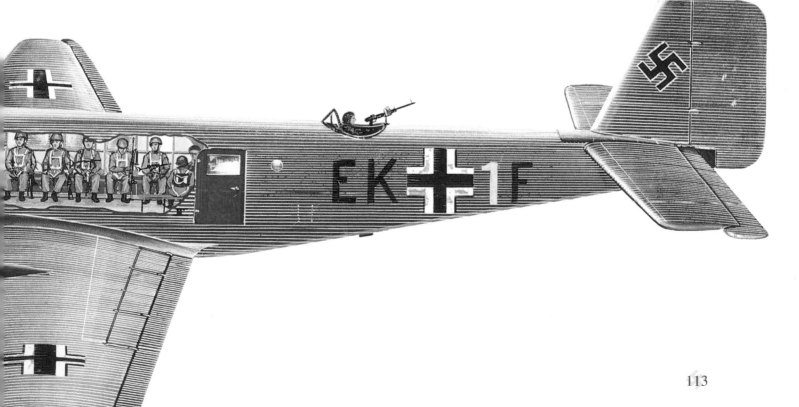

*Despite its technical obsolescence, the Junkers Ju 52/3m transport was one of many German aircraft that had to remain in service for lack of a replacement, and as the war lengthened, demands on this venerable type increased as its losses rose, presenting the Luftwaffe with a major headache as availability fell well below requirement.*

Against the Allies, other notables were Generalleutnant Adolf Galland, whose score of 104 victories was gained before December 1941, when he was appointed inspector of fighters and ceased operational flying, and Major Heinz-Wolfgang Schnaufer, who shot down 121 British aircraft by night.

In overall terms, 107 German pilots scored 100 or more day victories and a further two scored 100 or more night victories. There were also 22 jet aces, of which the highest-scoring was Bär, whose total of 220 victories included 16 scored in the Me 262. These successes are put into perspective by the fact that the highest-scoring British and commonwealth ace was Squadron Leader M.T.St.J. Pattle, an RAF pilot of South African birth who scored at least 40 and possibly 51 victories before his death in April 1941; the highest-scoring American ace was Major Richard I. Bong with 40 victories; and the highest-scoring Soviet ace was Major Ivan N. Kozhedub with 62 victories.

Even allowing for the incredible achievements of men such as Hartmann and Marseille, however, the figure that stands out above the others is Oberst Hans-Ulrich Rüdel, the sole man to be awarded the Golden Oak Leaves with

*Fuel supplies were always a problem for the Luftwaffe. As aggressive wars expanded the front line away from Germany, there were problems in ensuring adequate deliveries, especially on the Eastern Front where road and rail networks were completely inadequate, and then as Germany was forced on the defensive, Allied bombing eroded the country's ability to produce and deliver fuel.*

Swords and Diamonds to the Knights' Cross of the Iron Cross. A member of Stukageschwader (later Schlachtgeschwader) 2 'Immelmann' throughout most of the war, Rüdel flew a record 2,530 sorties (2,100 in a Ju 87 Stuka and the other 430 in an Fw 190) and was credited with nine aerial victories, with the sinking of the Soviet battleship *Marat* as well as a cruiser, a destroyer and 70 landing craft, and also with the destruction of 519 tanks (a world record) and huge numbers of artillery pieces and motor vehicles. What makes this remarkable tally all the more noteworthy is that Rüdel achieved his later successes after returning to action following the loss of a leg.

When Germany started World War II in September 1939, she had the world's largest air force of modern aircraft. Out of a total of 4,093, just over one-quarter of these were useful offensive warplanes (1,176 bombers of all types) for the type of *Blitzkrieg* warfare planned by Germany, and 1,179 were fighters (of which a mere 779 were single-engined fighters). However, it was the overall figure, or at least one similar to it, that was broadcast around Europe and added to the fear in which the German military machine was held. Yet it was the lower figures that represented Germany's real aerial

**Top:** *The Focke-Wulf Fw 190D retained the radial-engined appearance of the Fw 190A, but, as revealed by the longer nose section, was in fact powered by a Vee piston engine installed behind an annular radiator.*

strength, and even these concealed the facts that the Luftwaffe lacked adequate reserves of aircraft and trained aircrew, that German aircraft production was running at only a modest level (about one-quarter of what it would later become), that Germany was short of vital raw materials such as aluminium, copper, tungsten and rubber, and that the design and development of more advanced warplanes were continuing at a very low level of priority and then as a result of industrial pressures rather than government demands.

Overall, the Luftwaffe was adequately prepared and equipped for a short war, and only on one front. In the course of providing the army with excellent air support during the one-month Polish campaign, the Luftwaffe lost a modest 285 aircraft. Similarly, at the start of the Scandinavian campaign in April 1940, the Luftwaffe committed 80 aircraft and achieved decisive results largely through overawing its considerably smaller air force opponents.

The attack that was launched against the Low Countries and France in May 1940 followed the same basic pattern although on a larger scale, as the Germans mustered some 3,500 aircraft including 1,482 bombers and 1,264 fighters. Lasting nearly to the end of June, the campaign in the Low Countries and France was harder fought than either the Polish or Scandinavian campaigns, and accordingly cost the Luftwaffe heavier casualties in terms of men and machines. Nevertheless, the German air force achieved all its primary objectives in the course of an average of 1,500 sorties per day, and emerged from the campaign very satisfied with its performance. There can be little doubt, indeed, that in June 1940 the Luftwaffe had achieved its peak in terms of professionalism and strength.

All this was to change from the following month as Goering foolishly committed the German air force to its first strategic air campaign, entirely ignoring the fact that it was neither equipped nor trained for such a

The Heinkel He 219 Uhu was the finest night fighter developed in World War II, but was delivered only belatedly and in modest numbers as a result of political antipathies to Heinkel.

**Below:** The Blohm und Voss Bv 222 Wiking was a huge six-engined flying boat designed as a transport and then produced only in very small numbers.

campaign, in his desire to maintain the positions of the Luftwaffe and himself in the hierarchies of the German military and the Nazi leadership. This strategic campaign was the Battle of Britain, into which the Luftwaffe entered with the dual aims of destroying the Royal Air Force as a defensive and offensive force, and then of blockading the British coast and breaking the will of the British people with a bombing offensive, after which the German army, launched across the English Channel by the German navy, could sweep to victory under its accustomed umbrella of Luftwaffe tactical air support.

It says much of the core strength of the Luftwaffe that, despite its steadily increasing losses from July 1940, the overall failure of the Ju 87 and Bf 110 as warplanes against high-grade opposition, and the comparative lack of success of the Bf 109 once it was used as an escort fighter, the German air arm came within an ace of success as the losses of its bombers were proportionally lower than in the French campaign and the British were losing fighters and fighter pilots at a higher rate. In August 1940, for example, the RAF lost 338 Supermarine Spitfire and Hawker Hurricane fighters in combat, with a further 104 badly damaged, in comparison with the Luftwaffe's figure of 177 Bf 109 fighters lost and a further 28 badly damaged. More significantly, perhaps, in the decisive period between 11 August and 7 September, the British had to use part of its precious fighter

*The Messerschmitt Me 323 was the powered version of the Me 321 heavy transport glider, and offered the capability to deliver bulky loads to airfields virtually in the front line, but only at the price of a catastrophic vulnerability to fighter attack.*

*The Focke-Wulf Fw 189 tactical reconnaissance and close-support warplane was built in large numbers, and its extensively glazed central nacelle offered the crew excellent fields of vision in the battlefield role.*

reserve, which at the end of the period was a very low figure. Over the same period the RAF lost the effective use of many of its airfields in the south-eastern part of Britain as a result of Luftwaffe bombing, and was beginning to run out of pilots. During August and September, RAF Fighter Command lost nearly one-quarter of its pilots, and the flying training schools could not provide enough replacements with the skills that could be acquired only in operational flying. The result was that RAF Fighter Command's pool of pilots was approaching exhaustion, and from the beginning of September the Luftwaffe felt that the determination of RAF Fighter Command was wavering.

The battle was beginning to sway in favour of the Luftwaffe when the German high command intervened and, on the grounds that it was important to reduce Luftwaffe casualties by destroying British fighters at source, switched the offensive away from the airfields and air combat to attacks on aircraft factories and then, in direct response to a small British bombing raid on Berlin, to the heavy bombing of London. This had the effect of committing the Luftwaffe to long missions against a well-protected target, and of giving RAF Fighter Command a welcome respite to rebuild its aircraft and pilot strengths. The overall result was that the Luftwaffe lost all the gains made in the preceding weeks, and a revived RAF Fighter Command was able once more to exact an insufferably heavy toll of German warplanes that had to fly the gauntlet of RAF Fighter Command on their way to and from the target areas. Bomber losses soon persuaded

Goering, against the advice of his professional subordinates, to tie the previously free-roaming Bf 109 fighters to close escort of the bombers, which in turn resulted in poorer fuel economy and reduced endurance over south-east England.

Germany had lost the Battle of Britain by the end of September 1940, but refused to accept the fact in any other way than a switch from day to night bombing by unescorted units of the *Kampfgeschwadern*. This 'Blitz' effort was maintained to May 1941, but was unable to break the British as the Germans lacked adequate bomb-delivery capability for the effective implementation of a strategic bombing campaign. By May 1941, the night bomber effort had been trimmed from a high point of 44 bomber *Gruppen* to a mere four, as the others were pulled back for rest and rehabilitation before being transferred to the south-east and then to the east in anticipation of Hitler's next grand strategic moves – the Balkan operations and the invasion of the USSR scheduled for the early summer of 1941.

Despite its defeat in the Battle of Britain, the Luftwaffe was still a major tactical force, and for the Balkan operation against Yugoslavia and Greece the Luftwaffe was able to commit some 1,100 warplanes, which played their traditional roles of supporting the ground forces and paving the way for their deeper penetrations with 'terror raids' by bombers against targets such as Belgrade, which suffered the type of pounding meted out to Warsaw and Rotterdam earlier in the war.

The Balkan campaign ended with the airborne offensive to take Crete, and the success of this operation was sealed by the use of transport aircraft to fly in a major reinforcement of mountain troops and the success of the German bombers against the Royal Navy. The cost of the campaign was very heavy, however, and as a result Hitler decided never again to commit the airborne arm to such as operation.

With the end of the Balkan campaign, Luftwaffe units were moved to the east for the delayed start of the invasion of the USSR, which began on 21 June 1941 with an eastward offensive along the length of the new Eastern Front. For this campaign the Luftwaffe initially committed 2,770 aircraft in the hands of Luftflotten I, II and IV supporting Army Groups 'North', 'Centre' and 'South' respectively. Although the Luftwaffe faced Soviet air

*The Messerschmitt Me 163 Komet was a point interceptor with an extremely high climb rate and high level speed as a result of its rocket powerplant. The type took off from a two-wheeled trolley that was dropped as the Me 163 lifted off the ground, had very short powered endurance as a result of the engine's enormous thirst for its liquid propellants (fuel and oxidant), and suffered from a truly alarming propensity to explode if any residual propellants were jarred in a heavy landing.*

strength that was huge in outright numerical terms, the Soviet air threat was notional rather than actual as its aircraft were mostly obsolete and flown by pilots of poor quality. The result was a massacre of the Soviet air force, which lost at least 2,000 warplanes in the first 24 hours of the German offensive. In the short term, therefore, the German army was able to enjoy the virtually unhindered support of the Luftwaffe as it smashed deep into the western reaches of the USSR.

Gradually it became clear that this success was not total, however, for the Luftwaffe lacked both the warplanes and the concept of destroying the Soviets' production facilities for all types of weapon. The Soviet defence effort was initially hampered by a number of features, including the need to buy time for the evacuation to locations east of the Ural Mountains of all militarily important production facilities lying in the Germans' path, but gradually the resumption of production by these relocated production facilities allowed the Soviets to stiffen their defences as their own lines of communication shortened and those of the Germans lengthened. The weapons produced by the relocated production facilities were mostly obsolescent types that were already in production, but weapons of any type were better than no weapons at all, and the Soviet forces soon learned to extract the best from their equipment. The survivors gradually acquired a measure of tactical acumen, and as the factories started to produce ever-larger numbers of more modern weapons, the survivors from the original Soviet forces began to fight back effectively and to pass on their hard-won skills to fresh troops.

Thus the technical and tactical superiority that the Germans had enjoyed in 1941 diminished in 1942, even though the Germans were generally able to secure tactical command of the air over operationally important regions,

*Designed as a civil flying boat able to operate non-stop between Lisbon and New York, the extremely elegant Dornier Do 26 was used in very small numbers during World War II for the maritime reconnaissance and limited transport roles.*

*A real oddity that did not enter production or service, the Blohm und Voss Bv 141 was designed along asymmetric lines, with the extensively glazed nacelle offset to starboard and the boom carrying the engine and tail unit offset to port, in an effort to create a single-engined type optimised for the tactical reconnaissance and army co-operation roles.*

and by 1943 the Soviet air forces were approaching parity with the Germans in the overall level of their tactical capabilities, while benefiting from the advantages of a production system that turned out vast numbers of warplanes fully adequate for their purposes.

In 1943 the Germans belatedly undertook a number of strategic air operations with significant success, but by this time is was a question of too little and too late with warplanes that really were not suited to the task. In was in situations such as this that the organisation of the Luftwaffe revealed its major deficiencies, for even with the limited resources available it proved impossible to create a strategic striking force as the individual army groups to which the *Luftflotten* were attached jealously retained all possible air strength for the support of their increasingly fragile ground efforts.

The Luftwaffe made a final effort to secure air superiority over a major battlefield in the summer of 1943 with the Kursk offensive, that was the German army's last endeavour to regain the strategic initiative from the Soviets, and massed 1,700 warplanes for the offensive. This force achieved a number of notable successes, but was then checked and finally driven from the skies by the Soviets' huge strength of increasingly capable warplanes flown by better-trained crews.

For the rest of the war on the Eastern Front, the task of the Luftwaffe became untenable. Retreating constantly with the army units it was designed to support, the Luftwaffe continued to achieve success at personal and unit levels, but could not check the relentless growth in the number and capabilities of the Soviet air units. By 1944, Germany's bombers were all obsolete or at best obsolescent, and from this time onward it was left to fighter units – increasingly short of fuel and adequate pilot replacements – to check the relentless tide of Soviet strength.

Luftwaffe units were also posted to North Africa and Italy. In North Africa the success of the German air units generally mirrored those of the ground forces under Rommel's command, while those in Italy enjoyed short-lived success against the British island bastion of Malta and the Royal Navy in the

Mediterranean, but by the middle of 1943 the Allies had secured almost total command of the air.

The other theatre in which the Luftwaffe was involved in any major part was the Western Front. This had declined in importance during the early stages of the German invasion of the USSR, when sufficient forces were left in the west only to check the growth of British and later American tactical air operations over German-occupied northern Europe. When the Allies landed in northern France during June 1944, the Luftwaffe was able to fly only 319 sorties on a day in which the Allies put up many thousands of sorties, and could achieve no worthwhile results. Bedevilled by the demands of the Eastern Front, and using an ever-larger number of inexperienced pilots to fly obsolescent warplanes, the Luftwaffe units on the Western Front could offer only token resistance. A final effort was made on 1 January 1945, when some 750 German fighters were grouped for mass attacks on the airfields from which air support might be launched to support the Allied armies involved in the 'Battle of the Bulge'. The Germans managed to destroy some 300 Allied aircraft, which were replaced in a matter of days, but suffered heavy losses (including 150 pilots) and used virtually the last reserves of fuel available to the Luftwaffe. Operation 'Bodenplatte' (baseplate) can thus be reckoned as the last German tactical air operation of World War II.

Germany had fallen into all the traps of fighting a multi-front war. In July 1940 she faced Britain alone, but by the spring of 1941 had opened another front (the Balkans and North Africa that later became the Balkans and Italy), and then in the summer of 1941 added a third front in the form of the Eastern Front. The Luftwaffe, which had been designed for a one-front war of limited duration, was now faced by a war of extended duration on three fronts, one of them more than 1,000 miles (1,610km) long. On the Eastern Front the Soviets

*The Blohm und Voss Bv 138 was an extremely capable three-engined flying boat operated in the long-range maritime reconnaissance role.*

*The Junkers Ju 188 was a 'stretched' version of the Ju 88 that offered considerable capabilities but entered only belated development and production after it had become clear that the planned Ju 288 successor to the Ju 88 would be a total failure.*

burgeoned in numerical and tactical terms, and on the Italian and Western Fronts the skilled British were supplemented by an ever-growing American strength that very soon matched the British in terms of ability.

The German training establishment could not produce aircrew at a sufficient rate to replace losses, and the replacement crews lacked the quality of those they were replacing. Thus the strength and capability of German air units began to decline from July 1942, when the Germans could muster only 1,888 bombers and fighters for operations over the Eastern Front. Even though the belief that the war would be short had led to a postponement of the final development and production of more advanced warplanes, the production of current types did not expand fast enough to meet demand: in 1939 Germany's deliveries had averaged 217 bombers and 133 fighters per month, but by 1941 these had increased to only 336 and 244 respectively, and at a time when Germany's military commitments were significantly greater than they had been in 1939. Improvements became apparent in the year when Milch succeeded Udet: Milch advanced German aircraft production towards a total war footing, and during a 20-month period from November 1941 deliveries increased by 270 per cent from 12,400 machines in 1941 to 15,400 machines in 1942 and 24,800 machines in 1943. Production peaked in 1944, when 40,600 aircraft were delivered. By this time, however, it was not aircraft that were required, but the men to fly them and the fuel to keep them in the air: the supplies of both were wholly inadequate.

In was in this situation that the strategic bombing campaign of the Americans and British was decisive. The Nazi mind still demanded that air power should be used for offensive purposes, so the bulk of the available fuel was shipped to the ground fronts, and this played into the hands of the Allies, whose day and night bombing campaigns finally began to bear fruit in the middle of 1944 as Germany's industries and lines of communication were pounded mercilessly. An immense anti-aircraft artillery capability was created for the defence of Germany, and which at times exacted a heavy toll of Allied bombers, but fighter strength lagged far behind requirement: between February 1943 and September 1944, German fighter production rose from 700 to 3,375 aircraft per month, but the number of day fighters available for the defence of the Reich rose from a mere 120 in March

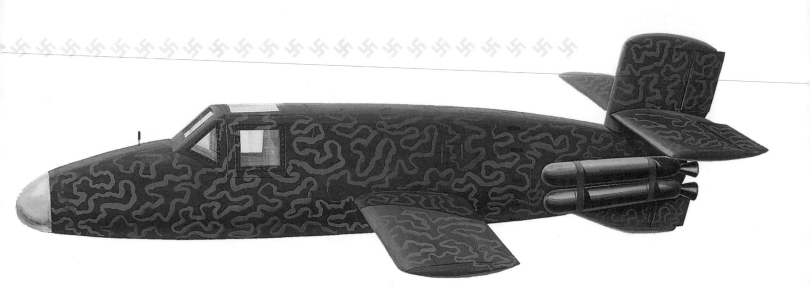

1943 to 475 in March 1944 and then declined to 280 in May 1944, when the American bombers were free to roam virtually at will over Germany with the aid of their North American P-51 Mustang escort fighters. The night fighter arm was able to muster a peak strength of some 700 aircraft against the British nocturnal campaign, and at times did manage to savage RAF Bomber Command, but could never offer a decisive opposition.

By the closing stages of 1944, therefore, the Luftwaffe was the palest of shadows of its former self which, in reality, had never been the force that German propaganda claimed.

*In the later stages of World War II the success of the Allied bomber efforts began to impinge so directly on Germany's attempts to sustain the war that all manner of expedients were tested and/or placed in production. The Bachem Ba 349 Natter (above) was a semi-expendable point interceptor designed for operation with a powerplant that comprised a short-endurance liquid-propellant rocket motor boosted during the vertical take-off phase by four jettisonable solid-propellant rockets. The armament comprised twenty four 2.87in (73mm) Henschel Hs 217 or 3hirty three 1.3in (33mm) R4M unguided rockets carried in the nose under a jettisonable cap. The Heinkel He 162 Salamander was a more practical interceptor with its turbojet engine mounted in a piggyback position above the central fuselage, and this trim little fighter was designed with a structure of non-strategic materials (steel and wood) and placed in production in a remarkably short time. The type suffered a number of aerodynamic problems as well as a tendency to lose parts of its wooden flying surfaces as a result of poor adhesive bonds.*

# DIE WAFFEN-SS

The Waffen-SS (Armed SS) was just what its title suggested, namely the armed branch of the *Schutzstaffeln* (protection squadrons) that started as Hitler's black-shirted bodyguard unit and developed, under the command of Reichsführer-SS Heinrich Himmler, into one of the most feared and fearsome organisations within the Third Reich. The responsibilities of the SS therefore increased from protection of the Führer to protection of the Nazi party and finally to protection of the Nazi state from all internal disaffection. Himmler was not content with this internal security role, however, and demanded the right to create the Waffen-SS as the SS's counterpart to the army for use in the land campaigns that would create and protect the 'Greater Germany'. The Waffen-SS was thus developed from its original role as Hitler's immaculately uniformed 'praetorian guard' into regiments and, early in World War II, into divisions that in turn proliferated into Panzer and infantry formations that were later grouped into SS corps and indeed, in the last stages of the war, into SS armies that had army formations under command.

As the war progressed, the initially rigorous recruitment standards of the Waffen-SS had been lowered to allow the enrolment of virtually any German, and then it was deemed advisable to open the doors to recruits of other nationalities so that the Waffen-SS could be portrayed by the Nazi propaganda machine as the cutting edge of an international crusade to wipe the Soviet system and state off the world map. The SS's 'foreign legions' were poor imitations of the German pattern, however, and therefore played a comparatively small operational role except, on occasion, against resistance forces in their own countries.

Since the end of World War II it has become standard to view the Waffen-SS mainly in the light of the undoubted atrocities perpetrated by a number of its formations, but this should not be allowed to disguise the fact that much of the Waffen-SS was constituted of formidable fighting formations.

The SS was the younger and considerably smaller of the two private armies created by the Nazi party in the 1920s, and headed from 1929 by Himmler it was nominally subordinate until 1934 to the considerably larger SA (*Sturmabteilungen*, or assault squadrons) that were commanded by Ernst Röhm as the Nazi party's street-fighting organisation. The tight-knit nature of the SS and its personal allegiance to Hitler were the main reasons it was used to emasculate the SA in the 'Night of the long Knives' in June 1934, when Hitler had become concerned about the threat posed by an increasingly ambitious Röhm. Although the SA remained in existence after this time, it

*The symbology and pageantry that was typical of the Nazi party as a whole was carried to an extreme by the SS, as typified by this street parade calling for recruits to the SS.*

was a body with a reputation rather than any real strength, and it was into this vacuum that Himmler moved as he started to expand the SS in terms of its numbers and power.

The Waffen-SS formally came into existence in 1933 as the *SS Leibstandarte Adolf Hitler* (Adolf Hitler SS Lifeguard), and in its formation can clearly be seen the distrust entertained by Himmler about the army, which he felt was a last bastion of the 'old Germany' and ultimately the only body with the power and the will to remove Hitler. For this reason, Himmler decided that the Waffen-SS must outshine the army in terms of the physique and smartness of its men and uniforms, for this would be a small but powerful propaganda weapon in the task of persuading the German people that the Waffen-SS was superior to the army.

The SS Leibstandarte Adolf Hitler was followed into existence all over Germany by the SS-VT (SS Reserve Troops) that were 'exclusively at the service of the Führer for special tasks in peace and war'. Like those of the SS Leibstandarte Adolf Hitler, the men of the SS-VT organisation were initially required to meet extremely exacting physical requirements, including an absence of fillings in teeth, and faced daunting demands in the exactness of their dress. Even so, applicants were numerous, and many army officers transferred to the new service for political reasons and for the fact that promotion could be gained more swiftly.

The third element of the Waffen-SS, a term that did not gain currency until the invasion of France in 1940, were the SS-TKV (SS Death's Head Units) originally raised as concentration camp guard units but also tasked with the quelling of any civil strife within Germany.

*Seen in February 1938, Hitler moves past a guard of honour provided by the SS Leibstandarte Adolf Hitler at a ceremony commemorating the burning of the Reichstag (parliament) building in February 1933. This act of arson was probably perpetrated by members of the SA and SS with the unwitting aid of a disturbed Dutchman of Communist leanings, and the Nazis were able to 'discover' in this a Communist 'plot' to start a revolution, which gave them an opportunity to persuade the aged President von Hindenburg to sign a decree suspending seven sections of the constitution guaranteeing civil liberties of various types.*

By 1940, the Waffen-SS totalled four units in the form of the SS Leibstandarte Adolf Hitler, SS Deutschland, SS Germania and SS Der Führer Regiments as well as the SS Oberbayern, SS Brandenburg, SS Thuringen and SS Ostmark Regiments of the SS-TKV, of which the last was the first 'foreign legion' as it had been raised in annexed Austria. The four main regiments had played a part in Germany's quasi-military adventures up to the outbreak of World War II, including the occupations of the Sudetenland, Austria and the rump of Czechoslovakia, and had started the process of being recognised as a part of the German military establishment. This did not please the army, for one of the reasons that it had supported Hitler during his rise to power had been the party leader's promise that the armed forces would be the only German 'sword bearers'. The army had therefore been pleased by the SS's emasculation of the SA, but became less satisfied with the situation as the SS expanded its military activities. The one solace available to the army, which was becoming increasingly adept at turning its face away from unpleasant realities, was its feeling that the SS was composed of parade-ground rather than real soldiers who would be revealed as poor troops should they ever see military action.

*The Nazi propaganda machine was able to achieve wonders with the image of the clean-cut member of the Waffen-SS.*

WAFFEN-SS

EINTRITT NACH VOLLENDETEM 17. LEBENSJAHR

The Waffen-SS was first committed to combat in the Polish campaign of September 1939, and the army savoured the fact that the SS Leibstandarte Adolf Hitler and SS-VT regiments did in fact perform poorly and suffered heavy casualties despite being subordinated to army units that provided additional support. Despite this fact, the realities of the political situation within Germany dictated that the sensible course (the disbandment of the Waffen-SS and the reallocation of its men to army units) could not be considered and the Waffen-SS was therefore upgraded and accorded divisional status even as additional divisions were planned.

The SS Leibstandarte Adolf Hitler was retained in strengthened form as a motorised infantry regiment, the SS-TKV regiments were grouped into the SS Totenkopf Division and men of the various police forces in Germany were used to create the SS Polizei Division, which was the first SS formation in which the originally very high physical standards were relaxed. There were men attracted by the Nazi ethos in a number of northern European countries, most notably the followers of Vidkun Quisling in Norway, Leon Degrelle in Belgium and Mussert in the Netherlands, and such men were used to create the first non-German SS unit in 1940. This was the SS Nordland Regiment that was soon followed by the SS Westland Regiment. In the same year, these two regiments were amalgamated with the SS

*Members of the SS swear personal allegiance to Hitler at a midnight ceremony at the Feldherrnhalle in Munich, the city in which Hitler had mounted the so-called 'Beer Hall Putsch' of November 1923 in his first attempt to seize power.*

*The 9mm (0.354in) Luger Pistole 1908 remains one of the most celebrated semi-automatic pistols ever created, one of the reasons for its virtual notoriety being the favour in which it was held by members of the Nazi party, for whom it was an item of standard personal equipment.*

Germania Regiment to create the SS Germania Division that was soon redesignated as the SS Wiking Division, and also in 1940 the SS Verfügungs Division was redesignated as the SS Das Reich Division.

The German invasion of the Low Countries and France in May 1940 involved the Waffen-SS and started the creation of two conflicting reputations: most of the Waffen-SS units performed well and began to acquire the reputation of being efficient military units, but men of the SS Totenkopf Division were responsible for the massacre of a number of British prisoners at Le Paradis, causing some concern within the army. Nothing was done to punish these men or to discourage further such acts, however, and the performance of the Waffen-SS in the French campaign resulted in the decision to expand the Waffen-SS.

*Surrounded by senior colleagues and behind a guard of SS troopers, Reichsführer-SS Heinrich Himmler harangues an assembly of the Nazi party faithful*

**Opposite:** *Hitler and Himmler are seen here at a Nazi party gathering.*

In September 1940, Himmler told the Waffen-SS that 'We must attract all the Nordic blood in the world to us so that never again will it fight against us.' But what was to be the definition of this 'Nordic blood'? Germany was to fight World War II with a large number of allies, including Finland, Italy, Hungary, Rumania and Bulgaria as well as a number of satellite states such as Croatia and Slovakia, but initially the description of 'Nordic blood' was limited to German citizens (Reichsdeutsche) and ethnic Germans of other states (Volksdeutsche), but the demand for additional manpower was so high that the title of 'honorary German' was introduced for anyone who might enlist.

Some 6,000 Norwegians and Danes enlisted in the Waffen-SS for service with the SS Wiking Division and a number of Freikorps (free corps), and these Scandinavian troops were allocated in 1943 to the new SS Nordland Division that was initially destroyed during the Soviet reduction of Berlin in 1945. There can be little doubt that the Scandinavians had real 'Nordic blood', and the same was deemed true of the Netherlands, whose men received the accolade of having the blood closest to that of Germans themselves: of all the non-German populations of Europe, it was the Dutch who provided the largest number of recruits for the Waffen-SS, figures of up to 50,000 being quoted. These men were used to create the SS Nederland Division, which ended the war trapped in the Kurland peninsula from which only a very small number ever returned. In theory, the largest contribution

was made by the Belgians, who were grouped into the SS Langemarck and SS Wallonien Divisions, both of which were seriously under-strength and were destroyed in the bitter fighting on the Eastern Front.

The Baltic states (especially Estonia and Latvia) provided some 22,000 recruits who were allocated to three divisions that ended the war in the Kurland pocket. Enough men were found in dismembered Yugoslavia and Albania to allow the creation of the ethnic Albanian SS Skanderbeg Division, the Moslem SS Handschar Division, and the Croat SS Kama Division, all of which were extremely poor in quality and were used only in what was effectively a Yugoslav civil war. Large numbers of Cossacks and Ukrainians were also recruited, suffering extinction on the Eastern Front, small numbers of Frenchmen were used to create the SS Charlemagne Division that was never up to brigade strength and was destroyed in Berlin, and tiny units of disaffected British and Indian troops were also created.

By the middle of 1941, the Waffen-SS had six divisions, most of them with German personnel. All six of these divisions were used on the Eastern Front, and soon displayed a genuinely excellent fighting capability. The SS Leibstandarte Adolf Hitler, SS Das Reich, SS Totenkopf and SS Wiking Divisions had suffered heavy casualties, however, and were withdrawn for

*This group of German 'top brass' includes, from left to right, Hitler, Hermann Goering, General Werner von Blomberg, General Werner Freiherr von Fritsch, Admiral Erich Raeder and General Wilhelm Ritter von Leeb.*

*Another pistol much favoured by the German military and political machines in the period of the Third Reich was the 9mm (0.354in) Walter Pistole 1938, another semi-automatic weapon intended as successor to the Pistole 1908 but in fact never more than a supplement to the older pistol.*

restoration to full strength and re-equipment with the latest weapons within a programme that saw a further expansion of the Waffen-SS to include seven full Panzer divisions. It was these formations that comprised the main offensive strength of the force with which Generalfeldmarschall Erich von Manstein restored a measure of stability to the Eastern Front during the spring and early summer of 1943 after the disastrous loss of the German 6th Army in Stalingrad: it was also the first occasion in which SS divisions were grouped into SS corps, and the success of these corps resulted in their employment at any point on the Eastern Front that was threatened by a Soviet breakthrough or where the Germans themselves wished to achieve a decisive superiority.

The success of these divisions under the command of von Manstein in February and March 1943 persuaded Hitler to accede to Himmler's demands for a further expansion of the Waffen-SS, which was now bolstered by the creation of the SS Hohenstaufen, SS Frundsberg and SS Hitler Jugend Divisions, of which the last was drawn from members of the 1936 generation of the Hitler Jugend youth movement and soon acquired a reputation for fighting skill as well as atrocity. The availability of these divisions also increased the 'fire brigade' role now envisaged by Hitler for the Waffen-SS, so the SS corps and SS divisions were used increasingly on the Western and Italian Fronts as well as the Eastern Front. The formation that saw the greatest movement was the SS Leibstandarte Adolf Hitler Division, which was moved between the Eastern and Western Fronts no fewer than seven times, on each occasion being required to move straight into action to repel an Allied or Soviet offensive. This tendency continued unabated between the time of Germany's disastrous Kursk offensive on the Eastern Front in July 1943 and the Allied invasion of Normandy in June 1944, when the opening of this third front finally persuaded Hitler that greater stability of deployment was required.

A side effect of the fighting success of the SS divisions that was not altogether useful to the longer-term survival of Germany was the fact that Hitler acquired a higher-than-merited appreciation of their leaders' command capabilities, and the result was the steady advancement to higher positions of commanders such as SS Oberstgruppenführer Josef 'Sepp' Dietrich, SS Oberstgruppenführer Paul Hausser, SS Obergruppenführer Felix Steiner, SS Gruppenführer Willi Bittrich, and SS Brigadeführer Kurt 'Panzer' Mayer.

*SS troopers exercise in Norway, the doctrine of the SS emphasising the importance of physical perfection and fitness as an adjunct to correct 'Aryan' thinking.*

Perhaps the most important of the 'fire brigade' battles fought by the Waffen-SS divisions was that which checked the British and Canadians on the eastern side of the Allies' Normandy lodgement in the summer of 1944: seven Waffen-SS divisions fought with enormous determination and great skill, preventing the development of the lodgement in this area even though it resulted in their own destruction. It was also in France that the Waffen-SS perpetrated two of the atrocities for which it will always be remembered, namely the destruction of Oradour-sur-Glane by the SS Das Reich Division and the massacre of 64 Allied prisoners of war by the SS Hitler Jugend Division shortly before its monumental effort to hold open the Falaise gap so that the 5th Panzerarmee, 7th Army and Panzergruppe Eberbach could escape the encircling Allies.

The last major effort by the Waffen-SS was the Battle of the Ardennes in the winter of 1944. The northern flank of the German offensive was entrusted to Dietrich's 6th SS Panzerarmee that included the four SS Panzer divisions of the I and SS Panzer Corps. Despite their high morale and excellent equipment, however, the formations of the 6th SS Panzerarmee could make little headway in comparison with the relative success of the army formations of the 5th Panzerarmee in the centre, and it was men of the SS Leibstandarte Adolf Hitler who were responsible for the massacre of 86 American prisoners of war at Malmedy.

The final list of Waffen-SS divisions included the 1st Leibstandarte Adolf Hitler SS Panzer Division; the 2nd Das Reich SS Panzer Division; the 3rd Totenkopf SS Panzer Division; the 4th Polizei SS Panzergrenadier Division; the 5th Wiking SS Panzer Division; the 6th Nord SS Mountain Division; the 7th Prinz Eugen SS Volunteer Mountain Division of ethnic Germans from

*The Waffen-SS was able to use its political strength within hierarchy of the Nazi party to ensure that it received full quantities of the best and newest weapons before the army.*

Hungary, Rumania and Yugoslavia; the 8th Florian Geyer SS Cavalry Division; the 9th Hohenstaufen SS Panzer Division; the 10th Frundsberg SS Panzer Division; the 11th Nordland SS Volunteer Panzergrenadier Division; the 12th Hitler Jugend SS Panzer Division; the 13th Handschar SS Mountain Division (1st Croatian); the 14th SS Grenadier Division (1st Galician); the 15th SS Grenadier Division (1st Latvian); the 16th Reichsführer-SS SS Panzergrenadier Division; the 17th Götz von Berlichingen SS Panzergrenadier Division; the 18th Horst Wessel SS Volunteer Panzer-grenadier Division of Hungarians; the 19th SS Grenadier Division (2nd Latvian); the 20th SS Panzergrenadier Division (1st Estonian); the 21st Skanderbeg SS Mountain Division (1st Albanian); the 22nd Maria Theresa SS Volunteer Cavalry Division (Hungarian); the 23rd Kama SS Mountain Division (2nd Croatian); the 23rd SS Volunteer Panzergrenadier Division (Dutch); the 24th Karstjüger SS Mountain Division; the 25th Hunyadi SS Grenadier Division (1st Hungarian); the 26th SS Panzergrenadier Division (2nd Hungarian); the 27th Langemarck SS Volunteer Panzergrenadier Division; the 28th Wallonien SS Volunteer Panzergrenadier Division; the 29th SS Grenadier Division (1st Russian); the 29th SS Grenadier Division (1st Italian); the 30th SS Grenadier Division (2nd Russian); the 31st Böhmen-Mühren SS Volunteer Grenadier Division of ethnic Germans from Czechoslovakia; the 32nd January 30 SS Panzergrenadier Division; the 33rd SS Cavalry Division (3rd Hungarian); the 33rd Charlemagne SS Grenadier Division (1st French); the 34th Landsturm Nederland SS Panzergrenadier Division; the 35th SS Police Grenadier Division; the 37th L'tzow SS Cavalry Division; and the 38th Nibelungen SS Panzergrenadier Division.

# Nazi Insignia

The head of the entire SS organisation was Reichsführer-SS Heinrich Himmler. Born in 1900 and a man of indifferent physical stature little according with the physical capabilities he demanded of other members of the SS, Himmler was the chief policeman of the Third Reich and in practical terms the second most powerful figure in Germany after Hitler. Himmler was appointed Reichsführer-SS in 1929, and was a close associate of Hitler. With Martin Bormann, Himmler was leader of a group of Nazi party functionaries known as the 'fireside circle' or 'midnight club' that took most of the

**1.** *Silver bullion cap eagle for officers*

**2.** *Cloth cap eagle for commissioned officers (silver thread) and non-commissioned officers (grey thread)*

**3.** *'Totenkopf' SS badge as worn on the Waffen-SS field service cap*

**4.** *Sniper's badge*

**5.** *Engineer assault boat coxswain badge*

**6.** *Reich Security Head Office (SS and Police Affairs Group) badge*

**7.** *Reichsführer-SS Personal Staff (Press and War Economy Group) badge*

**8.** *SS Economic and Administrative Head Office (Agricultural Administration Group) badge*

important decisions in Germany by isolating Hitler from contact with all but the most senior political figures and military officers. Himmler's authority in Germany was twofold: firstly he was a confidant of the Führer and thus able to exert enormous influence on the basis of this association, and secondly he had very great powers of his own as head of the Allgemeine-SS and Waffen-SS (the general and armed branches of the SS). Within the SS he headed the Reich Security Head Office and thus, via Reinhard Heydrich and later Ernst Kaltenbrunner as his deputies, the criminal investigation department under Artur Nebe, the foreign political intelligence service under Walter Schellenberg, the Gestapo (secret police) under Heinrich Müller, the concentration camp organisation, and from 1943 the uniformed police when he succeeded Wilhelm Frick as minister of the interior. Himmler saw himself as Hitler's natural successor, but was finally rejected by the Führer and then by his actual successor, Grossadmiral Karl Dönitz. Himmler was captured by British troops in May 1945 but poisoned himself before he could be brought to trial.

Although the German armed forces had only a small number of decorations to be awarded to their members, there were larger number of distinguishing and merit badges and other insignia for the armed forces and, most particularly still, the Nazi party and all its multitudinous sub-organisations. On the following pages are a selection of these badges not meant to offer a comprehensive selection but rather an indication of the awards that could be made.

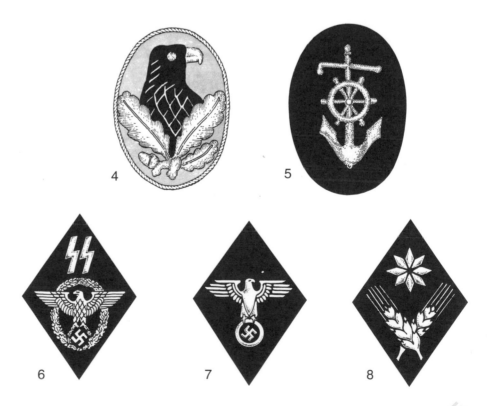

9. *Former member of the Hitler Jugend badge*
10. *Former member of the Ordnungspolizei badge*
11. *Former member of the Sturmabteilungen (SA) badge*
12. *Former member of the Auslands-Organisation der NSDAP (Nazi party) badge*
13. *Veterinary officer's and NCO's badge*
14. *Reichskommissariat for Strengthening German Nationality (Head Office Staff) badge*
15. *SS Head Office (Replacement, Procurement and Training) badge*
16. *Race and Settlement Head Office badge*
17. *Transport sergeant's badge*
18. *Marksmanship badge*
19. *Reichskommissariat for Strengthening German Nationality*
20. *SS Economic and Administrative Head Office (Economic Management Group) badge*
21. *SS Economic and Administrative Head Office (Building Affairs Group) badge*
22. *Signals personnel badge*    23. *Ordnance NCO's badge*
24. *Musician officer's badge*    25. *Farrier personnel badge*
26. *Medical and Dentistry officer's badge*    27. *Technical officer's badge*
28. *Administrative officer's badge*
29. *Security Service badge*
30. *Legal Branch officer's badge*
31. *Medical personnel badge*

24    25    26    27

28    29    30    31

*Below:* Himmler reviewing SS troops in field dress.

# Index